Returning to Happiness...

Overcoming DEPRESSION with Your Body, Mind, and Spirit

by Patricia Gaviria

Moving Energies

© PATRICIA GAVIRIA
© MOVIENDO ENERGÍAS / MOVING ENERGIES

"Returning to Happiness… Overcoming Depression with Your Body, Mind and Spirit"

Print Edition 2015
ISBN: 978-0-9910997-6-4
Published by: Moviendo Energías / Moving Energies - 2015
Boca Raton, Florida - Estados Unidos de América
movingenergies@live.com

This work is a translation of the original Spanish title:
"Volver a Ser Feliz… Venciendo la Depresión con el Cuerpo, la Mente y el Espíritu"; published in 2011.
Translated into English by author *Patricia Gaviria.*
Design of Cover, Interior, and Graphics: *Patricia Gaviria.*

NOTES TO THE READER:
- The subject presented in this book is not a Medical or Psychological approach; rather it is a subjective conceptualization based on the author's personal experience. Any professional treatment or medications used by the reader should not be suspended. The author and publisher do not take responsibility for any action taken by the reader after reading the content of this work.
- Some material from Patricia Gaviria's books is transcribed one in others. The intention of the author is, first, give respect to the already written concepts, and instead discard, better recycle them. And, second, because she is convinced that the same text read in different scenarios give the reader a new perspective and mayor comprehension of the subject.
- The content references The Urantia Book, 2nd Spanish edition, published by The Urantia Foundation in 1996.

This book is dedicated to those who one day, in their desperation and unfruitful search for hope, relief, and peace... took the unfortunate step to end their own lives.

CONTENT

- Dear Reader
- Introduction

FIRST PART.........15

Our Physical Energy at its Optimal Point / Our Physical Energy in Decreasing Space Levels or Frecuential Depression / How we can stimulate our Physical Energy and maintain its Optimal Point of Frecuency?

Chapter XI

Our Mental Energy at its Optimal Point / Our Mental Energy in Decreasing Space Levels or Frecuential Depression / How we can stimulate our Mental Energy and maintain its Optimal Point of Frecuency?

Chapter XII

Our Spiritual Energy at Its Optimal Point / Our Spiritual Energy in Decreasing Space Levels or Frecuential Depression / How we can stimulate our Spiritual Energy and maintain its Optimal Point of Frecuency?

Chapter XIII

Point of Balance Displacement / Reprogramming

- Goodbye
- About Patricia Gaviria
- Your Opinion is Very Important

Dear Reader
****

Sometimes when looking around it feels like nothing makes sense. Your emotions are perceived as strange; life appears complicated because you are without energy or the ability to face the problems that strike daily; and, on many occasions, the desire to continue living tends to vanish.

You hold the sensation of having fallen unexpectedly into a pond of cloudy waters, where you were thrown by circumstances that are very difficult to understand. Your arms and legs shake with vigor and your body weight pulls you towards the bottom of the water. The fear of being airless incapacitates you from coordinating corporal movements; and instead of finding even one light to guide the way to the surface where you can breathe, you end up completely exhausted and hopeless.

In the middle of the confusion you think you are alone, and although wishing to be afloat, you end drowning in the depths of an unknown environment.

But strangely, on some occasions, a great force surrounds and carries you to enjoy the scene unfolding above the turbulent and abysmal torrent. It seems like your face reaches the open space to take a profound inhalation, and in seconds your eyes glimpse a different world. There is light, breeze, sounds, and colors. Your emotions rise, the anguish dissipates, and staying alive no longer requires effort. The atmosphere is now warm and familiar; persuading you that this is the place where you truly belong.

And even if, once again, you feel debilitated, allowing the treacherous currents to drag you into the darkness and silence where a slow asphyxia suspends existence; keep hoping for an invisible and powerful hand will carry you to solid land forever.

Just hold onto the security that it will be so someday. Moreover, that day… could be today!

Introduction

****

Today I remember my husband's astonished expression while hanging up the phone, and his sad glance when sharing with me the news that he had just received: "Felipe, our dear friend, took his own life."

How could this be?

If less than a year earlier another of our "dear friends" had made the same decision.

How could this be?

If they were special young, healthy, and wealthy fellows with small children and beautiful families; if in the past, we all shared good moments and everything seemed to be fine.

How could this be?

The answer in both cases was the same: "They were depressed."

At that moment, I decided to tell my story. I promised myself that, somehow, I would narrate the process that allowed me to take a different path from

the one chosen by my forever remembered friends…
would introduce the *internal voice* that gave me the
strength to stay afloat during times of despair and
distress… would share the hope of living life with
courage, tranquility, and joy.

By writing this book, perhaps, I could touch the
hearts of people who are immersed in different
stages of the harmful situation of Depression.
Perhaps, my words would be the inspiration for them
to make some changes. Perhaps, I might offer a light
which guides them toward a new destiny.

It contains numerous elements: real memories of
particular, and even unusual, events that describe the
depressive condition from which I suffered over the
course of many years; philosophical analyses that
lead to an understanding of human nature; concepts
explaining the causes of depressive states, regarding
each one of the primary energy currents that
compose the self (body, mind, and spirit) and the
effects that are generated when they vibrate at low
frequency levels. In addition, I provide practical
advice in the use of natural and innate tools that
balance the physical, mental, and emotional aspects
of life.

I want to clarify that this approach is not
informed by fields such as Medicine, Psychiatry, or
Psychology, nor under any circumstance it is meant
to interfere with medical treatments the reader may
be in. Rather, it is based entirely on my personal
experience and a subjective theoretical
conceptualization, with the intention to offer an
alternative for those who are constantly searching for

a way to feel better and are ready to take practical, natural, and permanent measures.

To read "Returning to Happiness..." is a great adventure that I invite people to take; an opportunity that could be the starting point for a complete personal transformation. I congratulate those who confront the challenge because I am convinced that, like me, they will realize the human beings' true essence is to be well, and that overcoming Depression is much easier than they ever imagined.

Finally, I must thank especially my "Thought Adjuster" that has been the architect of my existence. To my beloved cousin, Elizabeth, who, with an open heart, accepted my help to make radical and regenerative life's changes. To my parents, for their love and unconditional support. To my husband and children, for being fundamental components of my progress. To my relatives and friends who offer me a warm environment. And to all those who collaborated in a special way to make this work a reality...

which I have faith, will inspire millions!

Patricia Gaviria

FIRST PART

ᖬᖬᖬᖬᖬᖬ

I will never forget the unpleasant sensation I had when entering the shady office of that eccentric looking Psychiatrist who was waiting for me on the other side of his desk.

When he asked: "What is happening to you?" My being gave a great sigh and fell into silence. How to answer the question that had been with me for so many years and yet had no explanation?

How can I explain "What is happening to me?" - I thought. "Where should I begin? How do I bring to light the things living inside me which I never had the courage to show, even to closest people? How long would it take to expose the stormy feelings in my heart and the thoughts tormenting my mind?"

I had to collect each piece of the puzzle of my life and position them one by one back into place. Perhaps it would be the only way to answer so complex question!

I
Magical Childhood

It is important to say that my first years of life were pleasant. I was born into a wonderful family (my parents and two brothers) in which love, tenderness, cordiality, and union were fundamental parts of our education. In addition, I grew up in a small city known for its friendly and open people, who offered me gratifying moments that will be in my memory forever.

Generally, I was a sociable, creative, cheerful, curious, and active girl. I loved music, art, dance, and, most of all, was passionate about learning. Regardless of the subject, my mind had thousands of questions and I tried to find answers no matter what; which led me to be a good student and always listening attentively to people who had something to teach.

While facing new matters, I handled insecurities with beautiful childish innocence. Like the fear produced when I thought the wool blanket, placed on the big armchair in front of my bed, was a scary monster watching me during the night.

Nothing prevented me from being open or expressing my feelings frankly to those around me. This allowed me to have a good connection with my family, made many friends, and even captivated some young boys' hearts who offered me a "just words" relationship because they were too shy to take my hand.

I always had what I needed. I even was fortuned to travel around the world which enriched me greatly. And the combination of all these experiences with my tropical, jovial, and full of contrasts -sometimes extremes- Latin culture, added a particular life point of view to my personality.

When I think about my childhood, many pleasant memories fulfill me. However, there is something that always catches my attention... something that from a very early age became part of my conduct, and it is a behavior common to most children regardless of race, gender, or nationality.

While playing alone, I would naturally and instinctively create a loud voice monologue, in which I asked questions and also answered them. However, it seemed like I was talking to another person; making many adults curious and ready to interrogate: "Who are you talking to?"

But, to be honest, I don't remember my response!

The only memory that I hold is that this self-communication was a game. A game that, little by little, not only became part of my daily life, but would also be a key element in my coming years of development...

Reflections of My Experience...

During my childhood I experienced the wonderful sensation of feeling free. Free to be what I wanted to be.

I learned that all children are born with innate and valuable tools necessary for proper development, and the correct use of those tools allows them to perceive an atmosphere that can be described as "magical."

From a young age, kids are ready with spirit and joy for life's adventure. Constantly, they explore their senses: listening, hearing, touching, smelling, and tasting everything that is new and draws their attention. Their curiosity is insatiable and their capacity to enjoy the simple and natural is enviable.

They know, for sure, they are an integral part of the environment.

Loving to be in action, they instinctively move in a rhythmical and recreational way. Music, imagination, humor, and self-expression (expressed through games, dances, or any pirouette their elastic bodies can handle) will make them feel full of energy and joviality.

Their goal is to always find something that makes them laugh... something that gives them thrill.

They are honest with themselves and others, having no fear of judgment; sharing with playmates of different ages, races, cultures, or languages without prejudices. They don't act with the intention to please or to force others to do exactly as they do; expressing without lies or masquerades, like when innocently they say on the phone: "My mother just told me she is not here."

They simply are, and let the world simply be.

They offer love and tenderness unconditionally; waiting for nothing in return and harbor no resentment against those who don't express the same sentiments. They are affectionate by nature, because they know people need love expressions to stimulate the spirit.

They give for the pleasure of giving and not for the pleasure of receiving.

They hold the incredible ability of going step by step, moment by moment, enjoying everything that arrives without worrying what will come later. When children want something, they simply go for it, free from anguish and fear. And when they have a dream, they know in fact life will give it to them, never questioning how.

Believing is not up for discussion.

Magical, yes, *magical* is the world kids conceive through their open minds and young hearts; allowing the universe's wisdom to guide and make them feel the true essence of existence.

"During my childhood, I learned that the little ones have the key to being happy and free... to being what they want, and what they must be."

II
Difficult Awakening

My life was normal and pleasant until I reached the first stages of adolescence -around twelve years of age- when, little by little, everything began to change.

As new experiences were faced, I perceived how I was leaving the "enchanted" world of my childhood and entering a different one, for which I was unprepared. Realizing I was an important piece in the great social system, my conscience started to understand I was a *unique* being that thought and felt like an independent individual. But, unfortunately, neither comprehending who I really was, nor having my own concepts about life or personal tastes that determined my way to dress, to speak, to act, to live.

The ability to openly express myself that I had during my early years was disappearing gradually, and I ended up moving around with shyness and concern. A feeling of insecurity, almost of fear, overtook me when I thought about showing others the new emerging individual who *"I"* barely knew. In addition, I assumed that everybody else understood the whole reason for living, perfectly confident in their desires and thoughts. Therefore, my self-confidence began to appear only when provided by others.

Simple choices, such as whether to drink soda, water, or juice... whether to wear the white or the blue dress... or whether to go to one place or another, created a huge mental storm that prevented me from making decisions. If someone asked me a direct question and waited for a specific answer, my heart would beat forcefully and my hands would dampen with the sweat produced by nervousness. My mind would be blocked and my voice would be mute.

I began, then, to walk with my head facing the floor, constantly evading people's glances; and my only relief was when I found pretty things lost on the ground. I also recall keeping my head down when boarding the school bus, saying "Hello" to the driver in a whispered voice, and while walking down the aisle I looked from the corner of my eye for the first seat available; wishing not to be seen or talked to and hoping to disappear!

In class, I didn't dare raise my hand when I had a question or comment, because I was afraid of being judged by my mistakes; of doing or saying something others would consider incorrect; of not fitting into the society I had been a part of in past days.

My developing personality was generating contradictory ideas and emotions, because I felt incapable of fitting into the social structure or managing my own convictions, firmness, and independence. It was how I began isolating myself in a world of very few participants.

But, as I say: "we never know when life is reserving us a surprise." The practice of speaking to myself when I was a young girl began to take an unexpected course. No longer were my own thoughts and words, but a second *voice* entered to be part of the conversation.

It was not what we know of as a sonorous voice because it was soundless; rather, there were vibrations placed in my brain, like if somebody was writing or typing information into it. These exchanges seemed like a pleasant chat with somebody else, during which I exposed my concepts about different subjects and received new ideas that should be processed and interpreted.

Was it the voice of my conscience? Tricks of my own mind? Just intuition? Or, perhaps, some special spiritual being who was next to me? I didn't know!

Fortunately, I was never scared. The process occurred instinctively and naturally, like when I was younger. It was such a comfortable sensation of peace and joy. Every night, lying on my bed, I anxiously hoped to communicate with this supposed *voice* that offered me hours of conversation; sharing my obstinate obsession to analyze life, question everything, and search for true answers.

As a result of these dialogues, I took a very different perspective on life: the people's behavior and way of thinking, the morality and religion I was raised with, the role of women in society, the real meaning of creation, and many other aspects that worried me. Questioning why suffering, wickedness, and inequality exist in our world or why so many good people like me couldn't manage to find peace, calm, and a state of complete realization.

Hundreds of the new concepts I was acquiring were very logical to me. Nevertheless, sometimes, they seemed so different and opposite from those expressed by the traditions of my developing third-world country's culture. I felt that I belonged to another world, far away from the one in which I was born.

With this special energy surrounding me, I was convinced something powerful, wise, and supreme surely exists... something far, but simultaneously near... something unknown, but at the same time familiar... something that speaks, but keeps silent... something to which I couldn't give a name at the moment, but, unquestionably, was a real part of me.

Day after day, this *voice* filled me with relief, and somehow became my companion and confidante. However, until then, I was very far from reaching an emotional tranquility and full understanding of what was really happening...

Reflections of My Experience...

In those early years of my adolescence, I understood that during our growth, the natural and innate factors indispensable for a life full of well-being are frequently blocked.

Many, and sometimes most, of the tools children are born with are disrupted by unsuitable systems imposed by society. When the young are exposed to concepts and habits so opposite their essence, they begin to change their normal behavior. Little by little, the joy disappears; there is no more space for imagination, self-knowledge, or self-expression; the meaning of existence gets distorted; and, especially, making contact with those universal forces that provide power and wisdom within us is no longer simple.

The reason lies in devastating events that occurred thousands and thousands of years ago. Humanity's way of thinking, acting, and feeling were affected, which generated an inaccurate and unstable base for the creation of future social, educational, and religious structures.

True and real aspects were mixed with false and unrealistic ones; creating great confusion that would interrupt our original connection to the rest of the universe. And, even if the world continued its evolution for centuries, overwhelming loads were brought to the present generations.

Today we are submerged in cultures with conditions far from those that human beings should be exposed. Children are forced to adopt abnormal identities in order to fit in, they lose the knowledge of how to interact correctly with others and with *Mother Nature*, and the internal communication with the divine energy disappears almost completely. So it is not a surprise that we continue facing facts that deteriorate our species, injustices hard to understand, genetic transformations and diseases that shouldn't be part of our being, and conditions that generate disturbing emotions. Sometimes, leading us to wonder how the mighty God allows all this to happen.

But, if we pay a little attention, we may realize that the natural instincts we were born with always stay latent inside us. Somehow, a bond with the force that preserves our original heritage still exists. And although it is beyond our knowledge to understand exactly what it is or who it is, we have to be convinced that this omnipotent energy is available for our evolution, or is at least ready for those who want to return to it.

Thus, for the young people who keep the essence of their origins and avoid adverse circumstances, life will unfold properly. Conversely, the ones forced to follow traditions that don't evolve, and learn concepts that go against their natural disposition, will develop troubled and unstable personalities.

Each generation comes filled with updated information from the previous one; and even if this is a key element for social progress, it is why many children's behaviors appear illogical to their parents.

Traditions are fundamental aspects of life; however, these should never obstruct the power that kids bring with their new and advanced ways of thinking and acting. Adults will always have the experience necessary for teaching, but they should never underestimate the universe's supreme knowledge, which leaves its trace on the beings that are born every day.

"In the beginning of my adolescence I understood that when kids are forced to change their original essence, they will have a hard time facing teenage years and it will be almost impossible for them to build a good life as adults. However, the relationship with the great universal energy may be suspended, but, luckily, can never be ended."

III
Confused Reality

In the following years, almost all the ideas I acquired through the conversations, seemed polar opposite from those the society had; so, unfortunately, anguish, insecurity, and a feeling of disorientation grew within me.

I began to perceive the world's indifference towards problems, such as misery, war, lack of education, physical and mental health deficiencies, and much more. My logic was overwhelmed when I saw children thrown in the street with no food, no home, no love, no life; how disrespect, violence, and death were interlaced in daily routine. And my heart cracked when the faces of good and worthy people had pronounced traces of resentment as a result of the constant fight against a system that denied them even one of the basic human rights: to learn how to sign their own names.

I noticed the beautiful and special essence of *woman* was repressed by a patriarchal society, where their freedom to act, learn, and achieve were denied. And they were forced to appear and, involuntarily, be the inferior gender. However, I knew if women could somehow recover their true values and innate strength, they would conquer and change the destiny of future female generations.

I recall carefully listening to the religious sermon every Sunday in church. Many things can be rescued from these gatherings, but, in general, most of my questions didn't have logical answers and other times I couldn't even get explanations.

I refused to accept the idea that the human race was created to suffer. That we learn and grow through pain and hurtful experiences; that we are paying for the guilt of some "original sin" committed long ago, and are condemned to carry a "cross" for the rest of our days if we don't feel remorse for something little understood. Or that God is very far away, reached only by saints, and those who do not approach that saintliness will sink into dark worlds of punishment and more agony.

I didn't think we are *sinners* as religion wants to teach us. Rather, I see us as *apprentices* beginning a long journey to acquire a higher conscience, and this status does not convert us into rejected beings that are punished by the universe.

I felt so strange and was incapable of sharing my feelings with anybody. I felt confident of my thoughts, but unconfident of my emotions.

Being sure we all have the right to find answers for our doubts, and because my religion did not manage to give me the expected support, I decided to walk different roads.

I embarked on studying the most influential religions preached around the world, but even so, none appeared to calm my restlessness. Then I explored Metaphysics, Spiritism, and Esoterism with activities like tarot, hand and tobacco reading, games to contact spirits, astral projections, and past-life regressions, among others. Unfortunately, the hundreds of new words and concepts such as karma, reincarnation, possession, or clairvoyance were not logical enough to clarify my confusion; producing a more intense mental storm and daze.

A difficult stage had begun!

My heart became aware about worldwide problems, yet I felt incapable of doing something to change it. An inner *voice* was accommodating my thoughts, but never answered questions as: Who or what was it? Where did it come from? Why, if it was part of my brain, at the same time, did it not sense like mine? And, even though my search continued with dedication, fear prevented me from asking these questions openly because I didn't want to be called "crazy."

Frequent strong headaches accompanied by nausea and vomiting started to paralyze me for days. I consumed lots of different pills to alleviate the pain; however, the normal doses quickly were ineffective, pushing me to reach for stronger medicines that harmed my body in other ways.

And if this wasn't enough, I had to confront new situations in the romantic side of life while discovering *love*. What can be, for most people, a pleasant and enriching stage, became a nightmare for me.

In front of the mirror I observed a barely developed girl, too skinny, with pale broken-out skin, and hair that looked like a used broom; displaying little attractiveness for the opposite sex. All my school years were spent at exclusively women institutions; therefore, a close encounter with an *extraterrestrial being* would have been simpler than communicating with a boy. I was the "Ugly Duckling" who nobody wanted to ask to dance at parties or even converse with for longer than half a minute.

The self-judgment turned into rejection and all this confusion redirected the course of my great searching.

Now, a desire, almost obsession, appeared in the form of finding *"Prince Charming,"* who would give me happiness forever, as shown in the most popular fairytales: Snow White and Cinderella. I thought if some protective gentleman paid attention to me, magically, the worried, timid, and anxious feelings would vanish. I was convinced my unhappiness was caused by not having *somebody* to show me how to enjoy life, motivate me, tell me I was pretty and intelligent, and persuade me that, yes, I belonged to the normal world.

But the more distressed I became about finding my rescuer, the faster the possibilities disappeared. Moreover, if the quest continued for the rest of my life, I would never find him.

At the end of this stage I faced many emotional shocks, and one of the most critical and delicate periods of my journey was about to begin...

Reflections of My Experience...

During these years of my development I comprehended that when we lack self-knowledge and self-esteem, we experience paralyzing and destructive conditions.

Millions and millions of individuals go invisible while facing society, incapable of expressing or acting freely. And most of the time, with displeasure, they end up doing what others want and playing the games imposed by social structures.

When resigning to construct our own personality and security, we sink into uncertain emotions that loosen our control on life and leave it in the hands of someone or something else. We accept inappropriate behaviors, provided that we don't feel rejected or despised... provided that somebody wants and needs us... provided that we may fit in the system. And if we do not obtain an unconditional acceptance from others, or at least their compassion, we collapse and think we are drowning.

We are easily convinced that, in order to have a space in the normal world, we must be good-looking and athletic; that only people with degrees, important positions, and wealth are winners; that we have value just fulfilling the requirements determined by a culture that has lost the authentic recognition deserved by all children of the universe.

So, despair and envy grow as we feel threatened by people who appear more intelligent, attractive or prosperous than us; creating an obsession with finding the perfect love, the perfect job, or maybe the perfect body that will satisfy this great space overwhelming our soul.

When our identity is shadowed, we build a life full of fear. Fear of being unloved, having less, abandoning yearnings and dreams; frightened of the future, of the death.

We learn to be scared and we get used to it!

It is necessary to be careful when searching for our own value and not to fall into an "egocentric" mindset. With this condition of learned behaviors we look very self-secure, but in reality there is an internal emptiness that has to be filled; so we try to control others by imposing our thoughts at all costs, wanting always to be right, emphasizing everybody else's weaknesses, and depending on constant praise.

This egocentricity is a distorted self-esteem, and it doesn't even come close of being true self-knowledge.

But it seems like the *internal voice* is a fundamental component in discovering our personality... it seems like this "whisper" opens the conscience not only to an outer world, but also to an inner one... it seems like she knows more about us than we do... it seems like she has a simultaneous individual and collective wisdom that teaches our true nature.

This is why the less we understand who she is, the less we understand about ourselves. And the more difficult the connection with her, the more complicated it is to have clarity of our individual identity and existence.

"During this period of my life, I visualized that self-knowledge and self-esteem are some of the most difficult aspects to acquire. But, maybe, the comprehension of what this *mysterious mental voice* is, or how she works in every person, could be the direct key to staying connected with our original essence."

IV
Limit of
My Reality

When I was about fifteen, many aspects began to extinguish the hope of finding the magical key, which would take me out of this emotional hollow into which I had fallen.

I was living in a world that nobody seemed to perceive, and, definitively, I didn't want them to perceive. In general, my behavior looked normal, but there was a constant internal battle where I fought not to feel what I felt... not to think what I thought... not to wish what I wished.

My family offered me a pleasant environment, but in my inner self there was just conflict. I wanted to scream and tell all of my loved ones how my life was; however, I thought they already had enough difficulties to also carry with my confusions and sorrows. I assumed this was a situation that could only be solved by me.

I envied the people who maintained their joy when facing serious problems, considering how difficult it was for me to be happy. Every inconvenience, regardless of how small, intensified the anguish and affected my ability to make decisions.

My main emotion was fear and any smile drawn on my face was faked.

When looking towards the future, my mind became cloudy and unable to identify what could happen next. There were no dreams, passions, or goals to reach. And even with great effort to succeed, I felt that I was completely incompetent and would always fail.

Being socially active and doing the things I enjoyed as a little girl became much more difficult. The distress increased. I didn't want to go anywhere or speak to anyone. When I was surrounded by a lot of people, my heart rate accelerated and my breathing almost interrupted; this is why restrooms became a safe zone when I wanted to evade this situation, and luckily they are available everywhere.

I started experiencing states I never imagined could be reached.

The early-morning hours turned very unpleasant; as soon I opened my eyes, a great and impossible to dissipate sorrow appeared. Slowness, fatigue, and apathy remained with me all the time, and accomplishing my responsibilities took superhuman effort. Usually I looked like a *sluggish* person, but the truth was my strength had to be double whenever somebody requested a favor or when something unplanned had to be done. I felt so guilty.

Now the bad humor was part of my daily routine, and, involuntarily, I focused on sadness instead of joy. Tears appeared without calling them. If somebody criticized or rejected me, I would fall into self-rejection, and the only way to find a little relief was sleeping; reaching the limit to stay in bed for entire days with a deep sense of frustration and grief.

Even my personal tastes began to change. The only clothes that called my attention were dark tones or black, and I felt incapable of wearing any bright color. When painting, I could only capture melancholic expressions or desolate gray landscapes. And it became more difficult for me to handle daylight, preferring to stay in darkness and silence.

It that wasn't enough, the constant physical discomfort took me to visit doctors frequently. There were no holes left in my body in which tubes had not been introduced to find the cause of my afflictions; nevertheless, the diagnosis commonly given in these cases was: "It is just stress, don't you worry."

I started to battle with two personalities: the one that pretended to be normal and the other that trapped me... the one that wished to continue and the other that wanted to sink... the one that understood and the other that was confused... the pleasant one and the unpleasant one. Sometimes, I blamed everything on my zodiac sign, *"Gemini,"* and the two-figured symbol it represents, but in the end nothing was logical. And less comprehensible was why that authentic, powerful, and wise *internal voice* could not manage to alleviate my condition.

Having the sensation of carrying a giant stone on my back, I was exhausted from constantly forcing myself to keep going on and pretending to be fine. I began to take the profile of a shy, serious, and unsociable young woman; beginning to think that I was really *crazy* and that there was no cure for my *madness*.

Many times I wanted to close my eyes and never open them again. The true sense of life was disappearing.

Today I recall a very particular day -after having one of those moments when emotions and logic clash- that I knew the limit had been reached. My body was not responding; my mind drove me crazy. I couldn't stand it anymore, and immersed in anguish and weeping, I had the cold determination… to take my own life.

Although it terrified me, I was secure and ready to accomplish my intention. I knew this action, considered by many people to be cowardice, would cause too much damage to my family; however, I thought that showing the real Patricia could be more devastating.

Luckily, the universe played its cards, and at the moment I was ready to take the most crucial step of my existence, the *voice* appeared again. But this time, it didn't speak. This time, it shouted:

- *"NO, NO! Stop! Please don't give up and listen!"*

Refusing to pay attention, I said:

- "I am so sorry, but I have to do it. I can't take it anymore. I am not able to continue. I am tired. Leave me alone!"

I lodged a feeling that exceeded all the limits of understanding; my mind was conscious, but at the same time completely out of reality. I experienced a force greater than my capacities, pushing me to stop going... to stop being; combined with the overwhelming mental vibration encouraging me to keep going... to keep being. There was so much tension between these two energies that I finally lost all vitality, collapsing against the floor and ending immobile and defeated.

The communication continued for a while, until I was calm. Today, I still remember part of the conversation:

- *"Have you had enough?"* – The voice asked.

- "Have I had enough? Of course I have had enough of everything, and that is why I am doing what I am doing." - I responded.

- *"In fact, what I am trying to ask is if you have had enough of looking for happiness outside yourself? Have you realized that the more you search for security in others... the more it goes away? The more you become obsessed with finding the truth in others... the more it vanishes? The more you under value yourself... the more others undervalue you? And when the sense of your own being is lost... the real sense of existence is also lost?*
Are you ready to turn around your life for good? It is your true will to change?"

- "Yes! But, I do not know how." - I affirmed.

- *"The first and most important aspect is the desire that your heart must have for changing, because nothing will be different if you don't decide that it should be.*

Second, take a sheet of paper and a pencil, and write WHO YOU WANT TO BE."

- "I never have known who I am or who I would like to be." - I responded.

- *"Just close your eyes and dream. It is not what others want you to be or what the circumstances have made you to be; it is how 'you' would like to be. Just imagine and write it. The strength and the wisdom are inside you. Trust your instincts and never deny the expression of your emotions."*

"If the raw material with which the universe has been created is love, balance, wisdom, abundance, joy, and perfection, and you are one part of the universe not more important that a sand grain but not less valuable than your own creator; then, how can you doubt that 'you' are also love, balance, wisdom, abundance, joy, and perfection?"

"When you recognize your foundation, and your body, mind, and spirit are placed in vibration with the primary essence... when you decide to be what you should be; only then will you begin to feel your reality. The truth is around you, but you listen and understand it within you."

- "If so, why do I feel so bad?" - I asked.

- *"Your own thoughts are pushing yourself far away from the original course, because you are refusing to accept who you are, denying your true nature, and blocking its flow."*

- "What do you mean by 'original course'?" - I interrogated.

- *"Imagine something. At the moment of your birth, you are sitting on a small anchored boat at the source of a great river of water that opens in front of you. Your eyes contemplate a canal shaping the entire torrent flowing ahead, and its image becomes part of the horizon after a long haul. The energy -in this case, the water- runs continuous and smoothly, with the necessary force to drag the boat in the same direction."*

"In the stage of growth, when your conscience is expanding and your first moral decision is made, the anchor loosens and your boat begins to follow the current's route. While navigating freely, you may observe, along the banks of the stream, thousands of small 'sites' -one next to the other- which get lost in the distance. Every location offers something different. You can contemplate and recreate yourself with an immense variety of beings, objects, scents, flavors, textures, sounds, thoughts, emotions, sensations, and much more."

"It is like a marketplace that you manage to explore in your watercraft."

"If you wish to take the paddles, move towards the shore, and get down in any of the dwellings that catch your attention, be completely certain that you will find something pretty. Each place visited will provide new supplies that may be kept in your ship

and will assure you a good trip… supplies that are essential for continuing down current until reaching the finish line of your river: The Universal Core."

"But, also, it is your decision not to get back in the boat; instead, continue walking and go deep into the forest that extends behind the sites. You will be, then, submerged in a strange land full of obstacles that are interwoven and prevent you from seeing the horizon; and although you try to bring them down, again and again, they will reappear. It is an environment in which the conditions are not appropriate, and will make you feel lost, weak, sad, and hopeless, because all the items you need to survive were left in your comfortable mode of transportation!"

"And if after crossing a great distance in this jungle, you encounter another river that flows parallel to yours, do not board any other boat that you see, since you will be following the pathway that has been designated for another person."

"Each individual has a unique space and their own course to get to the same destiny. And even if, in a certain way, you surrender to the current, it is your personal choice where you want to stop; what you want to feel, learn, or experience; and how long you are going to stay in each location before continuing the journey."

"You are the sole owner of your river and your boat; the performer of the action during your adventure. Furthermore, it is your choice whether or not to navigate this river and face this adventure."

"If you don't make a decision about whom you want to be, nobody will do it for you... not even the universe."

During that moment, a feeling of hope appeared like never before. Finally, I confirmed that the generator of my transformation was nearer from where I imagined: 'It' was within me. And even if it was still so difficult to understand *what* exactly 'it' was, I did not have any doubt that it had just saved my life.

I promised myself to never walk again with my head down. I would look straight into people's eyes without fear of being judged for whom I was or what I thought. That as much as I respected others, I would respect myself... that the value I gave to others, I would also give to myself... that I would put all my concepts in order and choose those with which I identified... that I would learn to follow my heart for recognizing my true desires, and, from then on, even if the trip was difficult, the courage would be my unconditional ally to find my destiny.

When writing *"who I wanted to be,"* I began to discover my own reality and experienced a lot of tranquility. But, the story of my life didn't end here. Many other events had to happen to generate the wonders of the years to come...

Reflections of My Experience...

During these years, I understood very important concepts.

We, humans, have exactly the same value as each of the elements that form the universe. But there is something that makes us very special. Something that offers us independence to decide who we want to be, what we wish to experience, and how to obtain it: FREE WILL.

It is our will to change or to be stuck in a stormy life. It is an individual decision to be sincere with ourselves or to sink in negative feelings that destroy the true reason for existence. It is a particular choice to fight for turning our dreams into reality or to be fearful when confronting any kind of failure. And, is an exclusive freedom to listen to the wise internal voice that shows us the correct way to achieve plenitude, or to continue with learned behaviors that prevent us from clearly receiving the messages that she transmits.

When we get connected with our essence, life is visualized in a more appropriate way. We understand that nobody gives us value; we are born with it. No one grants us the desire to be alive; it is part of ourselves already. Nobody can validate our thoughts; they are supreme and sacred. And don't forget that the force that makes our ideals a reality comes attached to our soul.

Also, I learned that happiness depends on personal determination and is not in the hands of others.

If we allow the truth and positive emotions to be lodged in our interior and healthily get our own respect, having somebody tell us "I love you" won't be necessary. We will not need stimulation to admire a flower, to be fascinated by a full-moon night, to vibrate with music that seduces us to move our body, or perhaps to loudly sing a tune that touches our heart, even if we sound like a record played by an old phonograph.

And if we establish that our joy is not the responsibility of others, we must also accept that neither are our *misfortunes*. Then, when difficult situations or negative people cross our path, we are the only ones responsible for letting our spirit be knocked down; for hiding under the wings of somebody else's thoughts and behaviors; and for searching for who or what should be blamed for our own inability to take control of survival.

A sincere desire is the base of any change, one of the most powerful tools that we have. To decide how to shape our personality and how to face life through the years is a privilege granted to us from birth; but the option to use this non-transferable *free-pass* is totally personal.

The true destiny of humanity is to enjoy a pleasant life. It is the reason we were created and for what we were born. However, even if it is sometimes difficult to accept, we are those who decide to cover our eyes... to close our ears... to seal our mouth... to chain our skin... and to repress our heart.

"During this period of my life, I confirmed that the greatest force of us humans is a powerful and wise energy that lives in the deepest place of our soul. But we have to make the individual choice to keep connected with it or to remain completely disconnected from it."

V
Returning to Be Born

Big changes occurred when I was approximately 17, which filled me with a lively sensation. And realizing the great power I had acquired, the connection with the *internal voice* became stronger.

My first impulse during this stage was to read positive-thinking and self-help books. Hundreds of excellent authors offer valuable information that teaches how to build self-esteem; and I am so thankful, with all my heart, to those who encouraged me with their writing at this point of my journey.

Day by day, I gained the courage to express many things that had been kept inside of me. I decided to speak, ask, and even discuss any subject. The most peculiar thing about the situation was that instead of being a shy, quiet, and insecure girl, I became someone who argued with great enthusiasm to prove my points of view. And if there is any doubt about it, my former high school classmates can vouch, as they surely remember me for all these attributes.

I felt like returning to be born. Now, I didn't worry of telling society about my new thoughts and how I would no longer accept many of its conditions.

Also, I remember the unbelievable happiness that came when I ended with the obsession of finding myself a rescuer. I had understood completely that the famous *Prince Charming,* for whom I had waited so long, didn't live in a distant kingdom, but he had his *private chamber* deep within my soul. Now when boys approached me, I showed an amazing sense of security in what I did and said; radiating a different energy that caught the attention of these young Casanovas.

I must confess. If anything took me back to feeling fear, it was when I finally got my most waited "first kiss" moment; which, thank God, I survived victoriously.

But, there was one last test that would confirm my newfound internal strength: the day a serious relationship had to be faced and my heart would be totally compromised. I was so worried my old habits would force me to blindly get attached to a partner. Happily, one more time, I attained victory; and when this first relationship ended, I had the strong resolution to continue my stimulating journey.

From then on there were many changes for me: a new personality, a new country of residence with different language and a better social system; new studies, jobs, loves, and friendships. The metamorphosis was so visible that even the old "Ugly Duckling" seemed to have transformed into something more attractive. I thank the universe for all those opportunities when I managed to enjoy life as never before.

At last, it appeared that all had gone back to normal. Like playing again in the magical world of my childhood, I was laughing, singing, dancing, and looking for incentives to keep me happy. I learned to trust my emotions and intuition started to play a big role in accomplishing my ambitions.

Well! Usually life is simple, but quickly it may turn complicated. When we think we know everything, we find that we just know a little something.

I thought discovering the magical key of my inner self would be more than enough to calm my soul; although, soon, I realized that occasionally the shadows from earlier years continued appearing as ghosts. Small details, such as comments, discussions, songs, films, or old memories, abruptly pushed me to deal with past conditions. After feeling a high level of joy, in a matter of seconds, I would fall into sadness and distress.

Oppression in my head and stomach made tears roll down my face, and the sensation of being a stranger reappeared.

I couldn't believe it!

It was impossible to give an explanation for what was wrong with me, so I persistently kept hiding this uncontrollable side of my existence from others. I got used to live no longer sunk in constant sorrow, but yet dealing with changeable extreme emotional states. One minute I was living; the next one I was dying.

So far, several acquired elements allowed me to feel better; however, I began to understand that many others were lacking. And with the exceptional aid of my inner force, which encouraged me to follow the course of my destiny, I was ready to persevere in the endless search for this *"something"* that could offer me the stability for always yearned…

Reflections of My Experience...

During these years, I recognized the meaning of a frequently heard expression, which, sadly, has become a *cliché* and lost its real value: "*LOVE* is the most powerful force of the universe."

There is not vocabulary enough to describe the concept of *love*, although, almost everybody can give testimony to the vigor and pleasure it generates.

One of the most special youthful states occurs when, for the first time, the mind becomes conscious of what the heart experiences. Suddenly, at the moment we are sharing with someone else, our being is transported to a world that offers calm and balance. It seems like our senses begin to fly and we perceive sensations beyond the surroundings.

Our eyes see things that we haven't seen before, our ears catch harmonies that have not been heard, our skin discovers impressions that we never imagined, and the heart lodges a joy difficult to exceed.

"Well! We are in love."

Again, we enter into a magical atmosphere. Comfortable aspects begin to flow naturally, such as tenderness, freedom, humor, cordiality, enthusiasm, and many other attributes that turn any sentimental relationship to "perfect."

And, of course, *love* is perfect. However, we humans have distorted not only its meaning, but the way we experience it.

We forget love is the energy or raw material with which the universe was created, and is inherent to humankind. From the moment of birth, we are, we experience, and we radiate this high emotion; and it can be verified by watching the image reflected by a new-born child.

Love is born with us and lives in us; it never departs and never arrives.

Unfortunately, as we grow, many unsuitable habits, ideas, and other factors are acquired that deny us the enjoyment of perceiving our true essence. And when somebody makes us feel the delicious taste of love again, we become confused and think this "sweetheart" is the real source of our pleasure; or maybe as the legend tells, we were crossed by Cupid's arrow and enchanted by its magical tonic.

This is why the day our *loved one* is gone, the charming current and the cozy state we had entered disappear. We experience a huge emptiness that brings opposite feelings; sadness, anxiety, humiliation, anger, and even hatred may become part of the difficult situation. So, we feel the impulse to bring the partner back and retain them at any cost, thinking that their company will bring the lost sensation of pleasure *one more time*.

"Love becomes possession."

Perhaps, we neither see in our own personality the same capacities and qualities we admire in our *soul mate,* nor feel capable of acquiring them; so we get blindly attached to the other person, looking for security and protection, being frightened of losing their support.

"Love turns into dependency."

Or maybe, when we don't even consider having love for ourselves and our self-esteem is too low, we easily become a puppet of anybody who expresses affection for us, disregarding disrespect and mistreatment. The self-value that we may have once had, is now in the hands of another.

"Love is transformed into shadow."

We must to understand that we cannot capture love, but only share it. "We really fall in love when I allow the love flowing through me to join the love flowing through you; there is no possession... no dependency... no shadow. So, there is no fear of losing this beautiful emotion that circulates within us, and which can never be taken away from our heart."

Nobody should have the weight or responsibility of making us happy with their love, much less be blamed if their hearts no longer vibrate alongside ours. In addition, if the loved ones have left this physical stage, let's just keep the good memories and not be drawn by the absence of what still vibrates in our soul.

Love's stream flows throughout everything that exists and fulfills us constantly. For this reason, it is very easy to fall in love with our own person; enamored with someone special who wants to share our life with respect and honesty, even if for a short time; enchanted by children, family, friends; seduced by the sun, water and wind.

"At this point of my trip, I learned that when we get conscious of *real love* and integrate it in all aspects of our existence, we will perceive the authentic connection with the creator's energy that wraps our being. It is when, truly, we return to being born."

VI
Depression?

The constant search for finding the cause of my afflictions continued with big changes and emotional falls. But, thank God, my inner support continued offering me some clarity to make important life decisions; like the day I wholeheartedly knew the boy with whom I had just had a pleasant conversation would be, in a not too distant future, my spouse and the father of my children.

I felt scared, cannot deny it. Nevertheless, I believed with confidence it was the correct choice and the appropriate moment to consolidate a relationship. And this is how, at my twenty-four years of age, back in my homeland and after one joyful and beautiful reception, I became *"Mrs. Patricia."*

I found somebody self-secure, active, happy, and mainly with a contagious desire for living. Filled with youth and loaded with dreams, we undertook the difficult task of balancing two independent, different, and completely obstinate worlds.

One tiny hope remained deep in my soul that I would finally be fine. But even if I was trying to enjoy all the good things that can be generated from being with a loved one, it was definitely very difficult to hide my uncomfortable situation. I didn't have a room of my own that could offer me shelter as I had in the past; I was no longer completely independent as during my college years; the internal voice was not my companion and confidant anymore, and instead, my new partner began to be my support.

The external pressures started to intensify!

How could I keep covering up or justifying actions that seemed absurd in front of anyone's eyes, including mine? Such as locking myself in a closet, crying because I didn't want to host some friends that we invited for dinner; feeling paralyzed when listening to all of the plans to go to some social event; staying in bed the whole day with a hideous body heaviness and an immense sensation of guilt; or perhaps when, frequently, without justification, an irrational desire came upon me to strike my head against the walls.

How incomprehensible it must be listening to someone who thinks nothing in life makes sense; who is completely insecure and doesn't know where to go; who neither laughs nor dreams; who is incapable of describing her emotions; and worst, who, despite loving and being thankful for everything she has, feels too tired to continue living.

Making an effort to defend some good things that I thought were still part of me, and looking for excuses to justify my *unexplainable* performance, instigated constant marital disputes and created an environment that was far from harmonious. This entire situation recalled my adolescence years and added one heavier than ever load: feeling for the first time that my behavior not only was destroying me, but also deeply affecting my husband. And this I couldn't stand!

Again, I sank into a hateful state and lost the little force that had taken. The anxiety pushed me to try one more time the frightful step I attempted in the past, from which I had miraculously been saved.

Even if my connection with the *voice* had greatly decreased, I held strong, and took a not so devastating but still drastic determination that seemed to be the last solution on my list: to visit a psychiatrist and be locked up at a mental institution, wrapped in a straitjacket. "What else can be done? Definitely, I am crazy and there is no cure for me." – I thought.

So my story continued!

I randomly chose a physician who I considered at that moment in my life to be a specialist in "crazy people," and requested an appointment. Today I recall the strange sensation I had when entering the dark office of that eccentric looking man who was waiting for me on the other side of his shabby desk.

When hearing the typical question: "Tell me what is happening to you?" I gave a great sigh and fell into a discouraged silence. How could I answer the question that was with me during many years and for which there was no explanation? How could I explain *what was happening to me?* Where should I begin? How could I bring to light all of the stormy things I never had the courage to show even to the dearest people to me? How long would it take to tell the complete story? - I meditated for a few minutes.

Thinking this was my last chance, I began to speak. But I believe only five minutes passed of me describing my complicated situation, when the doctor interrupted:

- *"Do not worry. I know what your problem is, and it is very easy to fix."*

I was astonished and believed my ears were failing.

- "What?" - I questioned with a surprised tone.

- *"DEPRESSION is what you have."* - The doctor said.

- "DEPRESSION?" - I asked.

- *"Yes. DEPRESSION! Have you ever heard this term before?"*

- "No." - I answered.

- *"You suffer from a condition called Depression. It manifests in several ways and yours could be classified as Maniac-Depressive. I am going to send you some medicine and, in around a week, everything will be fine."* - The doctor agreed, as he opened the desk drawer and took out a small box with caplets."

At that moment I felt such a hard impact from his words, that being hit on my head with a baseball bat would have been easier to handle. I couldn't understand what I was listening to, and as something unusual, a hearty laugh involuntary came.

- *"What happened?"* – He asked with surprise.

- "Are you saying something I have been struggling with for so long and putting all my determination to defeat will disappear in one week just by taking some pills?" - I questioned in a mocking way.

- *"Madam, listen. Please allow me to be sincere. When you came through that door, I never thought you would say what you just said. The situation you experienced generally drags people to fall into states of alcoholism, drug addiction, other disorders, or even confinement in psychiatric hospitals. I don't understand how you avoided these conditions and manage to look like a normal person."*

- "Doctor, with all respect," - I asked a little more seriously. "We are not talking about a *toothache* that may be calmed with an analgesic. Do you want me to believe that some 'pills' will transform my way of being, thinking, and feeling?"

- *"I see."* - The psychiatrist affirmed with a slight smile. *"You doubt the medication's effectiveness and will not use it, right? So let's make a deal. Promise me that, for at least seven days straight, you will take the pills and wait to see what happens. Please do it for me, if you don't want to do it for yourself."*

"One specific dose of the medicine has to be given to each patient. If there is not improvement with the initial amount, or if you feel worse, we may have to combine it with another prescription, until we get the right dosage.

Do not worry; everything is going to be fine."

- "Okay. If I accept, for how long would I have to take it?" - I asked.

- *"Indefinitely."* - He answered.

I didn't know what to think or say. For the first time, somebody was giving me a solution to my problem; however, it was difficult to absorb that I had a *disease* like many other people, and, perhaps, the only solution was to consume medication for the rest of my life.

Without a better option and barely excited, I decided to accept the deal.

I bought the supposed *"magical pills,"* which would fix the circumstances. In the beginning, my being fell into terrible states, even worse than before, but as promised, I called the doctor and he prescribed another medicine to combine with the first one.

With surprise, I began feeling better in a matter of days, as he foretold. My body recovered a great deal of energy and seemed less heavy. The anxiety and distresses were vanishing, and sadness no longer marked my face in such an abrupt way. In addition, like a blessing from the sky, the headaches disappeared.

At least the term "crazy" had been changed to "depressive," offering me some comfort and hope. Hope again… hope for finding the solution… hope for finally changing my life forever.

I cannot deny that for a long time the medications covered my condition and somehow stabilized me, but a large amount of negative symptoms remained hidden, and anguished thoughts continued bumping.

Sadly, without understanding the true sense of what was happening, my crooked pathway did not finish here either. Although the weight was lightened, I still needed to go through many events and to understand many more, to find an effective way that would pull up the problem by its roots…

Reflections of My Experience...

During this period I turned my interest to everything referring to Depression and started to learn about the subject.

I found that not long ago Depression was classified as a disorder or illness that causes instability in mood and behavior. According to medicine, it could be caused by an imbalance in some biochemical substance of the brain; it could be acquired by genetic inheritance, and even if managed, was very difficult to cure.

Under terms like bipolar, maniac-depressive, chronic depression, and others, the treatment of Depression was generally reduced to consuming medications. Eventually, a great variety of products began to be promoted in the market; prescribed ones, and others labeled "natural" that were supposed to induce *happiness*. And, in severe cases, extreme methods were used, such as electroconvulsive therapy that induces "electric shocks" to the patient's brain.

Psychology field also offered some therapies, but they were usually long term and accompanied with medications.

Even with all this information, there was not much clarity about the description, true cause, or an effective treatment to end this *strange* condition. So, based on all the years of experiencing it, I decided to shape my own concept of Depression in the following words:

Depression seems to be a set of negative manifestations that appear in the different aspects of a person's life; and, step by step, they affect not only the individual's development, but also the way they interact with the rest of the world.

Some of the symptoms are:

- Sadness and bitterness
- Constant desire to cry
- Anguish
- Fear
- Susceptibility
- Irritability
- Abrupt mood changes
- Heart Oppression
- Constant desire to sleep or insomnia
- Little appetite or extreme urge to eat
- Loss of memory and concentration
- Exhaustion and lack of interest in any
  type of physical activity
- Lack of sexual appetite or extreme sexuality
- General discomfort without specific cause
- Frequent headaches or migraines
- Hopelessness and self-rejection
- Tendency to magnify difficulties
- Solitary
- Pessimistic thoughts and feelings of culpability
- Desire to die and, many times, suicidal actions

A case of Depression may express only a few of the above symptoms, or conversely, most, if not all of them. The intensity may differ on a scale from slight to very intense. So, a symptom may quickly go from mild to extreme, or may change abruptly into an opposite one.

"In a matter of seconds a little blue becomes a deep sadness or a great joy in weeping."

I would divide Depression into two groups: the Justified and the Unjustified.

Justified Depression: The name says everything. This Depression has some *justification* because the person faces traumatic events such as: death of a loved one, physical mistreatment, serious disease, disability, bankruptcy, broken heart, or entering stages of great changes such as adolescence and elderly.

Identifying the origin or cause of *Justified Depression* is simple. And frequently the individual recovers, little by little, with professional aid or simply thanks to the reassuring touch of time, the natural life disposition.

Unjustified Depression: I would say, this one is very common and mostly affects modern society. Every day, in each corner of our planet millions of people -without regard for race, gender, or age- fall into depressive states for no apparent reasons.

Slowly and smoothly, the negative symptoms begin to interlace with people's personality, affecting their emotional and physical balance; and although sometimes some factors may be blamed for this condition, it almost always appears unjustifiable.

Unjustified Depression is very difficult to identify and is often treated only when it reaches extreme levels. Meanwhile, unfortunately, most people face *low* levels of Depression, preventing them from recognizing that there is a problem; even if, silently, it damages their physical condition, their perception of the world, and their social performance in an almost permanent way. This is why it is so common to hear phrases such as: "I am cranky and I never will change," "I always have bad luck," "I cannot find the course for my life," "Sadness and failure is who I am," and "Nothing makes sense."

However, we must pay close attention to the fact that *depressive states* have always been a part of humanity. Throughout history, a large number of personalities have taken their own lives in moments of hopelessness and confusion; many philosophers from ancient times offered their best words to describe "melancholy"; others, named *existentialists,* lived turbulent existences; and some are remembered as having died from *sadness,* submerged in great sorrows because of love.

All of this can lead us to think that seeing people full of problems, with conflicts and afflictions, a poor life attitude, and almost zero capacity to enjoy what they do, is something natural. We may even think the true role of mankind is suffering, distresses, and pain... that it is our essence... that there is very little to do... that the only way out is to simply continue holding on to this long existence and hoping its end will arrive soon.

Fortunately, for me, nothing of this was logical. It didn't make much sense to call a condition that displays such a wide, variable, and contradictory range of symptoms a "disease". It was not easy to accept that throughout history a high percentage of people have suffered from the same "disorder." Or how to explain why so many inhabitants from countries that face strong and prolonged winters are affected by depressive states, but, peculiarly, get better as the climate gets warmer? Or why a happy mom can fall into extreme sadness after childbirth? Or how such special beings as *children,* could be diagnosed with Depression, because they have been losing passion for life?

My heart kept telling me something was missing... something we were not understanding... something beyond conventional explanations that, perhaps, we had left back in human evolution... something we had to continue looking for, and maybe someday, manage to recover.

"During these years of my journey, I understood depressive states are common occurrences of our species; nevertheless, we do not understand them completely nor do we treat them in an effective way, so they continue running our lives and shadowing our destinies."

VII
Contradictory
Motherhood

In this stage, learning many aspects about Depression lightened part of the weight I was carrying. In addition, like never before and with more frequency, I began listening to other people who were also facing this disturbance.

It seems like being *depressed* was *in fashion.*

Although a kind of shadow remained over me, the medications I was taking managed to stabilize and relax me a little; allowing me to live life in the best possible way between work and marriage.

The connection with the internal voice remained debilitated, but I remember a very special moment when, in my mind, a determining affirmation appeared saying: *"You are ready... ready to be a mom."*

It could not be possible. If something I was afraid of was precisely being a mother, and, during times of sorrow, I considered never becoming one. How could I take responsibility for another person when I was not even able to face my own life? How could innocent beings be brought into this world full of pain and distress? How could the universe be telling me I was ready to be a mom?

As always, fear and confusion came back to me.

Immediately, mental images appeared of ladies with big tummies, *"Mrs. Ducks"* walking, and extreme behaviors with midnight cravings that drive husbands crazy; and the unmistakable silly faces of new parents overloaded with backpacks, bottles, diapers, strollers, and the inevitable "arsenal" to stay afloat in the complicated task of having a baby.

- "No! I am not ready." - I stated.

But a pleasant, magical, and difficult to describe energy surrounded me; making me acquire inner peace and a strong conviction that, indeed, I was ready, and very soon I would be giving birth. And thus -at 27 years old- I embarked on another adventure, bringing the whole family joy. After nine months of big-belly, walking like *Mrs. Duck*, luckily with just a few cravings, and a labor with several ups and downs, I became a mom.

Only a woman who has gone through pregnancy can understand the beautiful emotion produced by a little being growing and anxiously moving within her; wakening the maternal instinct, even if it is asleep, and causing any sensation other than love, tenderness, and amazement to fade away. We experience a fear that is not fear... a pain that is not pain... a special and powerful force, which, definitively, confirms that *yes* there is something beyond us in the universe generating the current where our boat floats.

To be honest, I never imagined feeling this incredible emotion of having my little girl in my arms, and witnessing the happiness she brought to our family's hearts. And even less, could I have dreamed, five years later, I would experience the same beautiful sensation when giving birth to my little boy.

As always, today I thank God for giving me the privilege to live the miracle of conception.

Lamentably, life is like a *roller-coaster*, which after being on the upper part of the track, falls again with so much power that it may terrify and often immobilize us. Because of my pregnancy, and other reasons I don't remember clearly, I had to suspend the anti-depressive medications; so, of course, combined with the joyful stage of being a mom, the negative symptoms returned, more overwhelming than before.

In the course of pregnancy, the female body not only undergoes an external transformation, but internally many of the vital organs must move to create a space for the growing baby. The child needs to absorb all the food their mother can provide and all the energy that she has available, even if it sometimes jeopardizes her own stability.

A tiny being that develops in our womb; feeds and breathes thanks to us; is protected by us; and in addition, at birth, takes away a part of us. So after delivery, it is common for women to experience a strong physical and emotional imbalance: nervousness, susceptibility, a constant desire to cry, tension, and let's not forget the confusion that the newborn requirements produce on the family atmosphere.

I remembered the anguish my husband and I felt about not knowing how to take good care of our children. We tried to read their minds to know why they were crying, and if our parental instincts failed, we fed them when they were cold and we covered them with a warm blanket when they were hungry.

So after two pregnancies, the fear, irritability, and impatience returned to mark my behavior. Incapable of understanding the world of my children, I was tired and without energy to follow their activities. It was a paradox; a contradiction. I was so happy for having my children, but simultaneously I felt overwhelmed by staying dedicated to the arduous task of being a mother all day long. I thought that, after finally beginning to enjoy life in its many aspects, I was now reduced to remaining within four walls, playing kids' games and forced to use an unknown childhood psychology.

Over the years my children were growing it was very difficult for me to create a calm home environment. I was trying to accommodate them in my world all of the time, because I was incapable of fitting into theirs.

I didn't want to feel overloaded with responsibility, but I did it. I did not wish to be in bad mood without knowing why, but, trying to relieve the frustration, I constantly looked for excuses. I did not want to think that I no longer had time to achieve my personal goals, but, repeatedly, I was questioning myself. And, much less, I did not desire to continue feeling this *existential distress*, but it remained, and I had no hope of tearing it from my heart.

The new medications were not enough to alleviate the anxiety. The relationship with my husband deteriorated. My children's behavior began to transform into defensive, disobedient, and aggressive. In general, the atmosphere in our home was perceived as heavy and tense.

Seeing how this stormy state was involving -as I expected- not only to my partner, but also to my two *little treasures,* hurt me. And only because of the love and respect toward all my dearest people, did I continue the arduous fight to overcome this situation.

I had to force myself to be a good mother and wife… to be a good daughter and sister… to keep myself alive.

A slight feeling remained in the deepest place of my soul that urged me to continue looking for a solution to this complicated problem, yet with disappointment. But what I didn't anticipate was that the universe would return to my rescue, and, very soon, great positive changes would begin. Those changes I yearned for so long…

Reflections of My Experience...

During these years, in spite of my exhausting situation, I realized that each stage of our journey brings an enormous and particular teaching.

If something exists that, by its own value, appears to be the most complete and enriching experience for us humans, it is *parenthood*. And when talking about being a mother or a father, we not only must think about people who are physically capable of creating a baby, but also about those who somehow are in charge of children and share with them the great adventure of their development.

Raising children tests us in aspects like sacrifice, discipline, dedication, and responsibility; raising children also gives us the wonderful opportunity to make contact with the creatures that radiate the *true essence* of our species and make us recognize how far we, as adults, have moved away from it.

Daily interaction with little ones shows us all the important tools left behind throughout our growth. They are the only ones who stand in contrast to our acquired attitudes that are putting us down to live in a world so different from the one we should... they, and only they, can demonstrate how incapable we have become of laughing, dreaming, loving, expressing, sharing; and, above all, searching for happiness with curiosity and persistence.

Often, some parents, hiding behind their work or individual activities, try to avoid raising their kids. But whoever foolishly wants to jump the task of supporting and educating children, life will sooner or later make them stand up to their own kids or someone else's, since the parenthood experience is a universal requirement in our evolutionary process. And this should not sound like a threat for those who run away from their responsibilities, but to make them realize that, although being a parent is one of the most complex experiences, we must face it with integrity and gratefulness.

Also, there is hope for individuals who, in this physical or material state, don't have the opportunity to be parents/guardians even if they wanted to, because they can be sure in another phase of existence, the universe will offer them a *second chance* to live and to take advantage of it.

"During these years, I comprehended that when we grow apart from the original essence, we create more conflict and distance from kids; and the more we want to force them to change their authentic and peculiar nature, the more we drag them, along with us, to enter the tangled jungle of this confused society."

VIII
The Beginning
of Change

Generally, when we experiment things that impact us with power, more significant changes take place in our thoughts and emotions.

My battle against negative aspects continued. And it was well after I turned 30 years old that, desperate to find solutions as always, I experienced an unusual event, relevant to the beginning on my great change.

At one point, a young clairvoyant and fortune-teller convinced me that the *voice* I had been listening and my confused condition were originated by a harmful and obsessed *spirit*, which was influencing me to take my own life. And although, deep in my soul, I knew this was not true; amid the desperation, I agreed to be part of a "cleansing ritual" that supposedly would alleviate my restless situation.

This is how I ended up surrounded by several people in a small room, with plenty of crosses, candles, images of saints, and many other pieces related to the "Santeria." Later, after some introductory words, strange events began to occur when the gentleman who was in charge of the event apparently was possessed by the spirit. His voice and behavior were transformed and he started to intimidate me with insults and threatening attitudes. Imperceptible forces made some of the objects fly through the air, and violently struck the young man several times against the walls.

Between shouts and weeping, other frightful episodes occurred beyond understanding, creating a feeling of panic and disorientation. At the end, the beaten man was left on the floor almost unconscious, and the tense atmosphere vanished when his conduct returned to normal. Supposedly, the undesired spirit had lost the battle and would go away forever, leaving me free of afflictions.

That night, we returned to the clairvoyant's house, and one of her friends *channeled* the energies of several spiritual beings that transmitted beautiful messages about my situation, offering a much more calm experience than I had had earlier.

Everything that happened was so confused and strange, and left me with great doubt about whether it was real or part of a horror movie. I tried to find an explanation from a variety of religious representatives and some other recognized people; however, their opinions and recommendations were so contradictory and absurd that pushed my condition to the edge... to the edge of an emotional breakdown that put me in a hospital emergency room, where, shouting and kicking, I tried to prevent the nurses from injecting me with tranquilizers.

On top of this, for the first time, my lamentable state was exposed to others. The mask had fallen; the secret had been revealed. Thinking everybody around would perceive me as an unbalanced person without a cure, produced so much more pain; but, thankfully, the unconditional support of my beautiful family helped me to retake the forces for continuing my heterogeneous pathway.

During the entire intensive search for solutions to my depressive episodes, this ritual was the most *radical and insane* action I had ever tried; and, certainly, was not the answer to the problem either. Nevertheless, I have to acknowledge that it gave me some ingredients to perceive in a different way the connection we have with other types of universal energies, and to be open minded and welcome the gift that was about to arrive in my hands.

And I don't have a better term than *gift* to refer to the book I received, by particular circumstances, after resting for more than one week and begging God for his help: "The Urantia Book."

"The Urantia Book" is a publication of more than 2,000 pages and almost 200 documents, considered to be the last-given and one of the greatest "revelations" to humanity. Transcribed around the middle of twentieth century, this masterpiece describes the origin, composition, distribution, and purpose of the entire universe.

After reading it, I understood our planet's controversial history. I understood the reasons why we erroneously think we are alone in this immense universe, the countless entities that compose the complex celestial order, the energetic circuits that connect us with the cosmos, the different states of consciousness that we acquire in our existential progress, the important role of human beings in this evolutionary race, and hundreds more fascinating subjects that satisfied my appetite for knowledge.

Finally, all of my questions had completely logical and convincing answers. Most of my concepts were reinforced and presented as truth, and many other new ones I had never considered, became part of my intellectual repertoire.

But, among all this amazing information, was something that deeply touched my heart; the description of the non-personal (pre-personal) highest spiritual element humans may receive: the *Thought Adjuster*. This device comes directly from God's energy and starts to work in each person's mind when the first moral decisions are made during early years of childhood. Loaded with exclusive information, it has the capacity to be associated with our intellect -if we allow it- and to adjust, uplift, and level off our concepts. It even has the sacred aptitude to wisely guide us for developing and continuing our spiritual evolution in the best way possible.

Most interesting was the explanation of how the *conscious* connection between human reason and the Divine Monitor engages in a "dialogue" that accommodates our ideas, logically and progressively. Although, when preconceived and erroneous personal concepts interfere with the complete understanding of the new ideas sent by the Adjuster, we may enter into states of great confusion.

Perhaps this was the *"lost link"* I was searching for... perhaps I was not playing with an imaginary friend and the harmful spirit who wanted to drag me down didn't exist... perhaps, this special and unique Adjuster, combined with other components that help mental progress, was the mysterious voice residing in my head from so long ago.

When all of this information matched with my own experience, and even if unacceptable for others, immediately became my truth. I realized that the *internal voice* I had tried to extinguish before was an ally instead of an enemy; and that I should *re-connect* myself with it. Finally, I had the big hope that now I would be more prepared to assimilate the conversations, assuring me that in fact I was not crazy!

The first thing I did was resume the frequent habit of searching for calm and pleasant places, for making contact not only with my inner self, but with other cosmic energies. Dusting off something had been trapped among the *webs* of forgetfulness for more than five years wasn't easy, and many days passed in a great silence.

Today, I remember one night being in company of my little daughter while she was falling asleep. When I was about to join her in the world of dreams, something resounded in my mind and shook me up:

- *"Do you remember, several years ago, when I asked you to write on a sheet of paper, who you want to be?"* - The voice said.

- "Yes!" - I answered, with great emotion.

- *"Now, I ask you to write: WHAT DO YOU WANT TO ACCOMPLISH IN YOUR LIFE."*

- "I really don't know what I want." - I astonished commented.

- *"If you do not know what you want, at least, identify what it is that you don't want."*

"While keeping the vision of what you really wish with tranquility and security, you will remain in your river. When the desire is interrupted with fear and doubt of achievement, your life will overflow into the dense jungles. When establishing your goals and yearnings, the universe will take measures immediately, for you to retake the course and experience your own existence."

"For so long you have been sailing in someone else's boat, and although it feels comfortable and many things have been learned, you must return to your exclusive destiny. Remember, people's paths must go parallel; never interfering with each other's and never using the same course."

"One of the purposes of existence is to look for your own truth; choosing authentic thoughts, emotions, and behaviors that offer satisfaction. And even if each truth is sacred, you cannot be mistakenly disrespectful trying to impose your beliefs on others, but neither to darken your own experiences by living the truth of others. Understand that you were created to be delighted with your soul's noble wishes; if they are not accomplished, it

is because you insist on denying what you are purely. Open your mind and heart and let your original essence flow."

"When you maintain happiness in living and enjoy simple things... when you learn to identify what elevates your spirit or what knocks it down... when you understand that the authentic sense of life is not exactly what we do, but how we do it... and when you expand your conscience, and identify your truth, fullness is experienced."

"Your truth will be recognized when you feel no fear, no doubts, no emptiness; otherwise, be sure that you still are very far from it."

I couldn't believe it. I was completely full of emotion and gratitude, seeing how this divine energy had embraced me again. And after thinking a while, I affirmed:

- "Yes! There is something I wish: to learn to be happy. To understand why I am depressed all of the time despite having so many pretty things around; to identify the real causes which incapacitate me from living, and find ways to overcome them."

- *"First, I want you to understand that you cannot learn to be happy, but you can return to being happy!*
"You were born with happiness within you, and simply have to be recovered. The negative things are illusions; the positive things are your reality. You decide which ones you want to confront."

"Second, all data referring existence is engraved in the cosmic circuits. The universe is the best teacher found in your road of learning; the one that stimulates your growth and development. Just get connected with it, and at any moment, you will obtain the answers you have been waiting for so long."

From then, I saw perfectly how I had been mistaken. I realized that the *internal voice* had never confused me; I had confused myself. It never left me; I had turned my back on it. And no one else but me had prevented it from trying to help me to improve my life.

I began to meditate daily and started to receive new information as when I was younger. Now, with fortune, I was better capable to freely and naturally participate in the dialogue, obtaining its true benefits.

It seems like an open water tap running a stream of ideas into my head that had to be processed by my intellect. It took several months of work and many getting ups during the night to write everything that was coming in, which had to be organized logically and interpreted in the morning.

To explain how all this information arrived in my *head* is a little complicated. I may just say the new ideas -introduced through the dialogues- were mixed with other ones I had acquired during previous years; and, perhaps, much more that had been covered by *"spider webs"* in the *"corners"* of my subconscious. In the end, somehow, the ideas were joined and gave me a very different approach to Depression than I had before.

All the puzzle pieces, randomly dispersed during my life, were put back together to show a complete image. And at last, a good overview could be visualized.

In the following chapters, I will try to transcribe everything I assimilated back then. It is not easy to explain such complex concepts that, maybe, are new for many of you; but I am convinced that when our minds are open to analyzing a wide range of ideas, we can better understand the processes of existence and produce regenerative changes.

SECOND PART

∿∿∿∿∿

Congratulations! You have reached the point at the journey of reading this book, where you will understand not just how I transformed my life, but also how you will manage to improve yours.

This perspective about Depression is probably very different from which you have until now. I don't know. What I am sure of is this is a particular, natural, and integral vision, and let me say, a much more *refreshing* than the traditional one.

"Particular" because it shows my own experience when dealing different depressive stages. "Natural" because it presents the fact that we are energetic creatures with an individual frequency that changes according to our life habits and the contact we have with the surrounding natural elements. "Integral" because the three essential energy currents of human beings -physical, mental, spiritual- are exposed with the conditions generated in us when each energy flow falls in Decreasing Ranges and loses tuning.

A vision which makes total sense for me and was a *decisive and irreplaceable* key to climbing out from the hole of Depression; the hole where I would never return!

IX
Understanding Depression

Depression is the set of negative conditions or symptoms acquired when our vital energies lose tuning as they enter into low vibration energetic ranges, different from our optimum or initial frequency.

I guess what you are thinking: "What? Pardon me? What did she say?"

But, don't you worry. I will explain this in a progressive way, and you will see it is much simpler than it sounds.

Let's begin with the basics...

Our Energy

It is complicated to expose the *energy* subject in scientific terms, so this is why I express myself in an elementary and sometimes metaphoric form.

To understand any aspect that refers to "existence," especially about human beings, it is necessary to consider a very important fact:

Absolutely everything that exists is *energy* manifested in infinite frequencies of vibration.

Energy means "life," which is described as the movement of the most essential particles in the universe called atoms. All atoms have a distinct oscillating movement named "vibration." And vibration can occur at different speeds -according to a specific period of time- creating the "frequency."

So, let's say for producing *life or energy* there must be movement… there must be vibration.

Now, imagine the center of the universe as a great volcano. From its wide crater, a gaseous, dense, and fine matter called "Universal Energy" constantly emanates; resembling a big cloud that slowly expands throughout space, like filling the infinite.

As it starts to move away from the volcano on a long journey, it manifests in diverse ways. Gradually, the speed, size, and position of the small atoms change; and as the distance among them increases, second by second, something new is created.

This is how every object, being, color, scent, texture, flavor, sound, and the rest of the elements, have a *unique* oscillation that allows each to display particular characteristics; similar to barcodes that identify items for selling or the fingerprints that determine the individuality of every person.

Everything, absolutely everything, in the cosmos has the same raw material, but is exposed in different frequencies of vibration; forming an enormous *spectrum* in which high frequencies diminish to low frequencies.

Elements of similar composition form smaller *scales*, equally arranged in progressive frequencies. For example, if we observe the "Light Spectrum" each color has its own place next to the others; delicately gliding from light to middle and then to dark tones. (See graphic No. 1)

Graphic No. 1

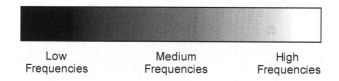

| Low
Frequencies | Medium
Frequencies | High
Frequencies |

Or, the flavor series begins with sweets, goes through salty ones, and then to acidic, according to their point of vibration. Sounds are manifested in high, mid, and low depending on their frequency. Solid elements have lower vibration speeds than liquids, and gases maintain even higher vibrations than liquids. Hot temperatures indicate greater oscillations; cold temperatures, smaller oscillations. Even living beings have ranges, some animals and plants distribute themselves in quick velocity and others, such as fungi, bacteria, and viruses are developed at very slow velocity.

And the classification can continue indefinitely.

Well, people are not an exception to this arrangement. After all, we also belong to the magnificent creation and enjoy an important place in this infinite arena of contrast.

The human species also has the "Universal Energy" as its essential matter, forming a particular scale or mini-spectrum where each individual occupies a position with an exclusive frequency. (See graphic No. 2)

Graphic No. 2

The moment we are conceived, the universe assigns us an *individual* space with a *unique* frequency, and our energy manifests in a completely original way.

The "Radio-Antenna" Effect

The fact that we are beings of energy vibrating in a particular frequency creates an effect that I call: "Radio-Antenna." We have the ability to *transmit* energy outwards from our body and, in addition, to *receive* energy from the external world. In other words, we are like "radio antennas" that handle one *private connection* with the rest of the universe.

Allow me to use an example in order for you to better understand:

Let's think about a simple manual radio: a non-digital device, without an automatic finder or "scanner" that has to be manually operated to locate radio stations. A technology from a not-so-old generation like mine, but which unfortunately seems almost obsolete in these days of fast communication. (See graphic No. 3)

Graphic No. 3

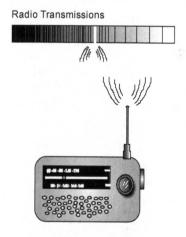

Radio Transmissions

The small radio consists of one *machine* supporting all the necessary pieces to catch the emissions spread throughout the air. The *power button* allows the machine to be turned on or off. The *antenna* can produce a range of waves with different frequencies, as well as capture waves generated by the stations. The *tuner knob* or *dial,* which moves from side to side, enables to locate the different available stations. The *amplifier* or *loudspeaker* reproduces currents caught by the antenna. The *volume* system gives the option of listening to the sound at various levels of intensity. And the *battery* or *cord* generates electric impulse for all the preceding elements to work properly, completing the transistor's purpose of broadcasting transmissions produced at great distances.

Now! As extraordinary beings, we behave in the same way as radios!

Our *physical body* is like the machine. Our *thoughts,* acting like an antenna, create different vibrations that connect with analogous emissions radiated by the Mental Energy, which flows throughout the cosmos. Our *free will* is the tuner knob we use to choose the universal frequencies with which we want to be in tune. Our *emotions* -like the music that sounds through the loudspeakers- are the result of the transmissions caught by our thoughts from the universe. How *intensely* or *freely* we express our feelings can be compared to the radio's volume. And the *stimulation* we give to ourselves to remain active, is similar to the battery or electrical flow.

In Tune

Let's say the radio is on and the dial is located at the point numbered "96.3 FM," which corresponds to a *classical music* station. The antenna begins to generate vibrations with the indicated frequency, and immediately connect to equivalent waves transmitted by the music station. This way, when the two radio-electric signals of exact frequency match, they open an aerial channel through which the smooth melodies are transported and later duplicated by the speakers at the intensity indicated by the radio's volume control.

If the classical music is clearly heard without any trace of sound from other stations or static, we can say the radio is "in tune." To obtain a true tuning, there are two conditions that need to be met: First, the machine has to receive the correct energetic stimulus from the electric system or from a fully loaded battery; and, second, the dial must be perfectly aligned with the indicator "96.3 FM," so the antenna can emit an equivalent frequency to the one transmitted by the radio station.

Exactly like radio-antennas, we humans have the ability to connect with three "stations," or universal energetic circuits, named: Material, Mental, and Spiritual. (See graphic No. 4)

Graphic No. 4

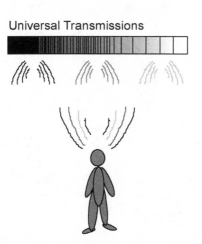

Universal Transmissions

At the moment of our conception, a spark of vibration is produced in our mother's womb, giving the initial impulse to ignite the "radio" and open the bridge or connection to the Material energy. Soon, as we grow and acquire a higher frequency, we perceive the Mental Circuit. And, finally, to catch the Spiritual station, we must reach a point of much greater vibration.

Here is when we consider that human beings are not *uni*-dimensional, but *tri*-dimensional, because we are the interaction of three powerful currents of energy that must work together in complete coordination. (See graphic No. 5)

Graphic No. 5

And at the same time, each current vibrates at an independent frequency, with unique functions and characteristics. As follows:

- *Material Energy*: we may visualize it as a "red" colored smoke cloud expanding through the great space. This current manifests our physical body, allowing us to perceive the external world with the senses of smell, taste, hearing, touch, and sight.

- *Mental Energy*: we can think of it as a "yellow" colored cord where all the memories of the universe are registered. It gives our brain the material to generate thoughts, ideas, and concepts, needed for us to understand how to interact and survive in the physical world.

- *Spiritual Energy*: we may imagine a beautiful "blue" colored river of energy; a channel through which we connect with much-higher frequencies than those offered by the Mental Current. It offers the most altruistic and noblest ideals of our existence, and expands our consciousness so we can distinguish correct from incorrect, real from unreal, truth from illusion, life from expiration.

In the next chapters, I will present more deeply these three primary or essential energies.

Meanwhile, let's say that as radio antennas, our machinery (body, mind, and spirit) must produce *equivalent* vibration frequencies to each one of the three main currents, in order for us to get in tune with them.

The good condition of our body is subject to a correct vibrational level of the Physical Energy, offering us vitality and health. The appropriate performance of our mind depends on the right flowing of Mental Energy maintained by the brain, bringing us an agile and creative intellect. And our spirit is fed by the amount of information circulating through the Spiritual Current, flooding us with the higher wisdom that directly arrives from the creator's force.

We are pure energy connected with central universal powers by way of specific frequencies. But we must be in tune with them to catch the necessary information that will assure a suitable corporal, mental, and spiritual performance.

Out of Tune

If for any reason the electricity or battery is not giving enough power to the radio, the transmission we are listening to begins to lose connection and gets distorted. Or if the *dial* has been moved, even a millimeter, from the exact frequency, the components of the music start to fade and harmony is replaced by a rainy noise. This is when the radio goes "out of tune."

In the same way, if *our* energy changes the original and correct frequency that produces the connection, we will enter into an interference field and will fail to keep communication with the sources. If our being does not maintain a specific amount of energy or our battery goes down, we begin to lose all the positive aspects and perceive others instead that produce confusion and distortion of reality. Our "inner fire" starts to extinguish.

Consequently, the physical body runs out of vigor and begins to form strange conditions like diseases. Thoughts, ideas, and concepts no longer flow easily, leading us to make incorrect decisions that affect our good social performance and an appropriate interaction with the world around. Likewise, the bond with *God* starts to disappear, causing us to misinterpret life's true sense and perceive ourselves to be abandoned, anguished, and without hope.

If our vibration is suitable, we will receive positive stimulation from the universe; but if our vibration is unsuitable, we will lose it.

Now, to better understand how we get out of tune from the universal forces, it is necessary to speak about something I call *Frequential Space.* It is defined as the area, section, or energy field each existing element occupies in the spectrum to which it belongs.

If we use a piano instrument as an analogy, we can visualize every one of the "keys" as a *Frequential Space* in the "keyboard" scale.

Each *Frequential Space* or *Field* is formed by three internal parts:

1- *Midpoint or Optimal Point:* located in the middle of the section and is where the element energy vibrates at 100%. (See graphic No. 6)

2- *Decreasing Space:* field that extends towards the side of the range in which frequencies decline. Here, the energy waves generated by the midpoint or core of the element lessen in intensity until vanishing completely in the next Frequential Space that precedes the spectrum.

3- *Increasing Space:* field that expands from the midpoint towards the direction of the scale where vibrations rise. Here, the energy waves of the element gradually increase in intensity until arriving at the adjacent Frequential Space.

Graphic No. 6

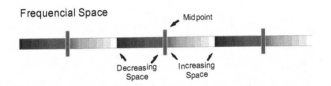

Let's go back to the radio communication example!

In the wide range of communications, every radio station is assigned to a specific aerial strip to transmit its own information. Each station acts as a Frequential Space, having a midpoint at which the emission is transmitted in an integral and perfect way, and two adjacent areas where the signal starts to lose all its qualities.

In same way, radio transmissions are caught by radio devices through frequential fields.

If the radio is tuned to the correct frequency "96.3 FM", of our favorite classical music station, the sounds will be vivid, clear, and exact. But if we move the button toward the side of lower frequencies, a rain of noises begins to distort the *purity* of the original sound. The melody progressively vanishes, the instruments disappear one by one, and the volume intensity lowers until the connection is completely finished.

If, delicately, we continued moving the knob in the same direction, the next Frequential Space will be reached; bringing us new sounds from a different station, perhaps a sports network, which has its radio channel "95.8 FM" beside the classical music broadcast.

Now, returning to the classical music station, but this time we continue moving the tuner knob toward the other side, into higher frequencies, the previous phenomenon will take place again. Little by little, the signal of the classical tune will be lost, until the information transmitted by the adjacent frequency "97.5 FM" is reached, which in this case belongs to a *News* station.

So the classical station's Frequential Space begins at the point where sports are broadcast, continues until tuning is perfect, and ends in the other side when the news zone interposes.

The beautiful symphony loses all its original core components when on one side is replaced by the commentator's shout of "Gooo…oaal!" that announces the local soccer team's score; and, on the other side, by the voice of the analyst giving an "economic report."

When its vibrations are diminished, or by the contrary over-stimulated, the music gradually becomes noise; until it stops being music… until it disappears.

And, once more, we must look at the wonders of human beings!

In our corresponding dimension and as creatures of energy nature, we are also manifested in Frequential Spaces.

We express an essential center or *Optimal Point* of frequency when our energy vibrates in an integral condition or 100%; a *Decreasing Space,* in which our vibrations decline until 0%; and an *Increasing Space,* in which our energy raises until the limit to be off its own place… off its own manifestation. (See graphic No. 7)

Graphic No. 7

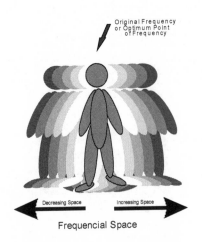

Original Frequency
or Optimum Point
of Frequency

Decreasing Space   Increasing Space

Frequencial Space

As I already explained, everything works well if our energy vibrates in the exact frequency of the universal sources. But if our energy goes out of tune, our personal conditions will change.

If we don't stimulate ourselves properly and our vibrations go down into the Decreasing Space, the symptoms of "Depression" appear one by one; affecting our lives in many ways. Or, if by other circumstances, we *over* activate our vibrations up into the Increasing Space, different stages of "Stress" will be faced that are equally harmful for the balance of our beings. (See graphic No. 8)

Graphic No. 8

DEPRESSION

STRESS

Whichever the case, the more we move away from the *Middle, Optimal, or Original Point* of frequency, the more our body, mind, and spirit lose the connection with the primary sources.

I want to emphasize this: *if we don't stimulate our energy to a suitable degree, we will be out of tune.*

And, if we stimulate ourselves disproportionally, we will also go out of tune.

When we move from the Optimal Point of frequency, our nature dissipates and becomes deformed. The positive forces decrease; the real is transformed into something unreal. And if the vibrations reach the edge of either side of our own Frequential Field, our raw material will be forced to take the last step: simply, stop being.

In this book I focus just on "Depressive" stages, because all the material related to the "Stress" zone is a subject for another publication.

Vibrating in Decreasing Space

The decreasing section of our Frequential Space is composed of hundreds of levels, and each generates a different negative condition for us.

Using the decimal scale as a reference, we might say that the center of our body is number 10, which handles the highest frequency of the Decreasing Space. The lower levels in the scale would be assigned numbers 9 through 1 correspondingly, and the last stage, where the field ends, would be number 0.

100% of the positive aspects of life's spectrum vibrate at level number 10. In this way, all information necessary for the body self-builds and maintains its good operation; all true thoughts that produce pleasant emotions; and all altruistic concepts that allow self-growth, are available gifts for us if our energy keeps the frequency at this level number 10.

But with each step we go away from being in tune, a positive aspect is lost and the opposite negative aspect is gained; at each diminished degree of energy, a constructive element disappears and a destructive one takes life.

In level number 9, we live 90% of the positive aspects and begin to experience 10% of the negatives. In stage number 8, we tune 80% of the positive aspects and gain 20% of the negatives. And, thus, we continue in a proportional count down, until arriving at number 0 where we completely lose the capacity to feel any positive vibration, and catch 100% of the negative ones.

For example, if my body frequency is kept in level number 7, only 70% of the correct energy will flow through me, and the rest will be out of tune. I will have an acceptable physical condition, but sooner or later, those parts of my body that are out of the right vibration, will begin to fail. Or if my frequency stays in number 3, I will feel heavy and weak all the time; only 30% of my body parts will respond properly, and the rest will progressively lose their correct operational capacities.

Something similar happens with Mental Energy. If my brain frequency is at number 8; 20% of the information will be lost, and my emotions will be slightly negative. Or if I drop my mind to a much lower state like number 2; 80% of my thoughts will appear confused and distorted, bringing devastating feelings constantly.

The same process occurs with the Spiritual Energy.

Depending of the amount of vibration given to our energy currents, we will feel the intensity of their benefits. The approach to the Optimal Point of frequency is *directly proportional* to favorable, healthy, and useful conditions; but the distance from this midpoint, is *inversely proportional* to them.

So we may say depressive states appear when Physical, Mental, and Spiritual energies vibrate at any frequency below number 10. And according to the position at which we remain in the Decreasing Space, different personal characteristics will be noticeable.

Let me show a general perspective: many people are accustomed to their vibrations being at not-so-low levels (for example number 9 or number 8). They usually believe the few negative aspects that manifest are an integral part of their personalities. They are individuals who, although not mired in sadness, barely laugh. They have enough energy to carry out normal responsibilities, however, their bodies feel heavy and dislike physical activity; and even if they seem healthy, are vulnerable to illness. They get used to living with a little of emptiness... a little of bitterness... a little of pain.

For people who usually vibrate at numbers like 6 or 7, discomfort and affliction is normal; presenting neuralgias and chronic pains. They develop unsociable, pessimistic, and irritable temperaments; handling insecurity and low self-esteem. They feel uncomfortable with changes and new adventures... they feel victims of the world.

In levels like numbers 4 or 3, stronger symptoms begin to manifest. People lose desire to do any type of physical activity. Sadness and anguish remain. The senses fall asleep. It is almost impossible to maintain a good performance in their relationships or work. Also, self-rejection and an inclination for dying appear.

In lower planes, as numbers 2 or 1, individuals remain asleep for long periods of time, their coordination fails, and body movement is almost impossible. They exhibit total disinterest towards normal dynamics and responsibilities. There is no desire to eat, listen or speak.... there is no desire, even, to be touched. The negative situation becomes too overwhelming and the desire to take their own life increases.

At the last step, number 0, contact with life's source is almost exhausted. The agony and desperation are inconceivable. There is not a bit of desire, sense, or hope. States outside reality are experienced, in which everything is perceived cloudy and turbulent. And a strong force appears to be preventing the person from continuing... from existing.

Unfortunately, the farther we move away from the attraction energy produced by the core of our being, the less connection we have with life. And if we go below level number 0 all bonds that unite us to the Essential Energy are lost; passing into another state of frequency, out of our rank of existence.

Depression

As we have seen, Depression is a subject that cannot be looked upon from only one point of view. It is necessary to understand it and treat it from three aspects: body, mind, and spirit.

Remember, we are born in tune and natural instinct urges us to stimulate our energy. But as we grow, negative situations, habits, and conditions have to be faced; changing our vibrational level and pushing us to experience low frequency sensations out of our connection range.

Inadequate life habits of diet, exercise and resting; harmful practices like drinking, smoking, or drug use; and/or other conditions such as noise and pollution, have caused many people to stimulate the body poorly or overload it uncontrollably, carrying the Physical Energy beyond its balance point.

Closed and radical religions; overcrowded environments that generate deficient education systems and arbitrary events; devastating and sensationalist news focus by the media; and others, generally push us to *think* in the negative. We sentence our Mental Energy to be out of tune, and, sadly, we create a habit of it.

And keeping our mind far from its Optimal Point reduces the possibility to make contact with higher energies of wisdom, to generate positive changes, and to elevate the spirit; dimming the transformational miracles offered by the Spiritual Energy.

For this reason, most of the time, it is so difficult to have a good life performance. We lose self-security and don't manage to take correct pathways that will give us happiness. We assume mistaken approaches with our kids, choose inappropriate people to share with, and take jobs that don't fulfill our personal expectations. We create pain, confusing thoughts, unhealthy emotions, problems, and sufferings that are not required for our evolution. We feel incapable of taking control of our own destiny.

Yes! We are definitively surrounded by infinite aspects that throw our vital energy into depressive states, placing us in a world that lacks logic or sense.

In later chapters, I will explain how each of the three primary currents work, what happens when they are out of balance, and how they can be stimulated to recover their correct flow.

For now, let's conclude:

"Depression is generated when personal energy vibrates in Decreasing Space frequencies; and gradually, some or all of the physical, mental, and spiritual components necessary to maintain an ideal development are lost."

Memories of My Experience...

Honestly, it is very difficult to explain how I felt during this period of my journey. The information that arrived in my head was too much and needed to be understood; nevertheless, everything began to make sense, convincing me that I was neither crazy nor ill as I had been told.

For some reason, in the course of growing, my three energies left the Optimal Frequency I had when I was young. Being in the interference levels became a habit, preventing me from seeing and feeling life in a clear way.

Thus, the insecurity only occurred when I blocked security; I was seized by fear just when the flow of tranquility was cut; and sadness marked me when I shadowed the joy. My vital currents were out of sync... my light was extinguished... my internal fire was consumed.

But I understood that complicated steps or too much work were not required to balance my three primary currents. Only the simple, normal, and innate tools of my nature had to be rescued, which would stimulate and maintain my energy into a correct place of vibration.

The first requirement to recover *my raw material original state* was to have a deep and sincere conviction for changing. Fortunately, I was willing to place the *batteries* into my *radio* and begin listening to the assigned stations; to open the "windows" of my being, so a new "breeze" could enter and refresh my body, mind, and spirit; to leave the past behind and undertake the present that would generate a different future ahead.

The second condition was to adopt correct habits and behaviors that would accommodate my essential energies. This way I could:

- Develop a much more resistant body and improve my health.
- Reprogram my mind, so I could return to thinking in a completely positive way and remain open to talent, creativity, and logic.
- Create a favorable atmosphere where the spiritual current could fit, elevate, and extend my conscience.

And third, I had to accept that feeling "well" was an entirely personal task of perseverance and dedication, with absolute effectiveness.

That it did not matter how much I wracked my brain trying to find those *"responsible"* for my imbalance and immobility or how much I continued fighting the outside circumstances, feeling like a victim of the "evil world" and its "wickedness"; because, I will always find not just one, but tens, hundreds, or thousands of elements on which the weight and guilt of this situation could be placed… a situation that definitively, was in my hands to transform.

I decided not to focus on problems, but on solutions. Exploring different methods for how to stimulate my Physical, Mental, and Spiritual Energies, one by one; I would be able to exchange many of my old habits for more effective ones to unblock myself.

In this stage, I understood that to make real changes and obtain happiness was so much easier of what I had thought. If the Universal Energy was a source of just positive aspects, and when I move away from it, the negative ones come; then, the only thing I had to do was take practical measures, letting the essence flow to connect myself... to tune myself. The rest would be in the universe's hands!

Such as when my body is oxygenated and activated while breathing rhythmically and I enjoy the benefits of air without even being conscious of the process. But if my nose and mouth are covered with a very tight bandage, soon my body reacts anxiously. I begin to feel distressed and fight to breathe; I go out of control, more and more, as my breath is exhausted. When the only thing I have to do is remove the bandage, give a great sigh, and let the air do its work. What can be easier?

And thus, I "finally" started the exciting journey of recovering one of my gifts from God: the base of our material expression... the First Original Current... *the Physical Energy...*

X
Our
Physical Energy

The Material Energy is the prime or basic substance that supports the whole universe; a "red mist" that gives origin not just to our physical bodies, but to the rest of perceivable elements surrounding us.

At the moment we are conceived, a portal or *window* is opened in a specific place on the universal spectrum. Immediately, increasing vibrations connect with emissions transmitted by the universal material current; generating a channel through which the raw material and information or data necessary to build our body -with characteristics maybe similar but never the same as another being- are captured.

The universe's force gives us a beautiful and perfectly coordinated physical device, equipped with sufficient components to delight us with infinite sensations and to survive the space and time adventure.

Our Physical Energy at its Optimal Point

After the fertilization "spark," and thanks to the *mother's* direct stimulation, the energy gradually increases its vibration. Thus, some part of the body manifests at each level of frequency through a progressive process, until all the corporal range is complete.

Cell by cell, tissue to tissue, muscle after muscle, organ by organ appear smoothly and delicately, before reaching the Optimal Point of frequency assigned for each one of us in the spectrum.

Like an apple tree that, thanks to the excitation produced by solar light and earth nutrients, at certain parts of its branches begins to increase the vibration. Then, one small green fruit is created, which grows as vibration increases. Not only does its size change, but also its color; from the "green" frequency it rises to the "red" frequency. Also, its skin begins to shine, its interior goes from hard to soft, and its flavor turns from bitter to sweet; until the apple reaches a point where it is *ripe* and in excellent condition to be consumed.

Likewise, when we manage to tune our Physical Energy to the correct frequency, all the corporal pieces acquire the essential data to work at one hundred percent (100%). The heart, brain, lungs, and every other organ offer their particular service in an effective way. The blood along with all chemicals and fluids run with suitable speed and volume. The senses are completely activated; eyes, ears, mouth, nose, and skin are ready to react to any environmental agent our body detects. The skin appears fresh, the hair shiny, and nails and teeth solid. The corporal weight keeps proportionate, facilitating mobility and flexibility.

Maintaining our exact frequency of vibration creates a general state of vigor, effectiveness, and balance. We feel alive and may run, jump, dance, and sing. There is neither a pain nor slowness; only well-being and freedom. We radiate an aspect of vitality, health, and beauty.

Our Physical Energy in Decreasing Space Levels or Frequential Depression

I want my dear reader to pay close attention to the following paragraph: "*All elements in nature tend to lower, slowly and progressively, the internal vibrations of their own matter, if they are not activated by some external stimulus that maintains its frequency in the Optimal Point.*"

If we use again the example of the *apple tree* and raise this question: "What would happen if the juicy fruit is taken from the branch and left for many days outdoors on the ground?" We will find that without the activation provided by the tree's nutrients, the vibrations of the essential particles of the apple begin to decrease.

Little by little, the texture becomes wrinkled; the skin loses its brightness; the flavor goes from sweet to acidic; the color fades to brown tones; the contour lines become deformed. And it arrives to a position so low in oscillation speed that it ends up rotting, because organisms able to be developed in low frequencies -like insects and bacteria- appear and start to consume it.

The general aspect of *agreeable and healthy* happens to end in *disagreeable and unhealthy!*

Analogously, at birth, we lose the direct support offered by our mother's body. And if later in life we do not activate our energy correctly, our internal vibrations will decay in progress. One after another, each physical body part slows its own oscillations, damaging the functionality in an opposite sequence to which it was manifested.

The organism that was built in an increasing succession starts to deteriorate in a decreasing way. Organ by organ, muscle after muscle, tissue to tissue, cell by cell, they go out of tune and get *unprogrammed*; exhibiting conditions opposite to those that gave them life.

When the activation is incorrect, we feel heavy and lose mobility. Our joints stiffen -like the hinges of a door that is never opened- and pains and neuralgias increase. Our muscles become flaccid. Our appetite is lost, and the corporal weight is drastically altered, changing the natural and aesthetic figure.

Our glands fail to produce the hormones indispensable for a good physical performance. Our heart lowers its power and diminishes the blood pressure necessary to properly irrigate the entire body. Our internal PH begins to change from alkaline to acidic. And even the brain fails to process the Mental Energy accurately.

As the vibrations diminish, our capacity to enjoy the sensations offered by the world around also decreases. Our senses more easily perceive negative impulses than positive ones: we see ugly when pretty; we taste bitter when sweet; and the touch of any hand no longer causes pleasure, but revulsion.

Our skin becomes opaque and withered, our hair loses its natural brightness and mobility, and our aspect is perceived as haggard. In addition, when very low vibration levels are reached, microorganisms of low frequency, such as bacteria and viruses, come alive; developing infections or diseases that can sometimes be devastating.

In general, the balance and coordination of the corporal system begin to collapse. And similar to thousands of processes that have occurred for the creation of our physical matter, thousands of such processes go in an inverse way; bringing harmful conditions for our state of health.

Our body, little by little, stops being a body, and the adventure of living begins to lose its enchantment!

Let us not forget, our physical substance must constantly have a specific impulse *equal* to the frequency assigned to us when we are born; "a generator, a battery, or an electrical current producing the necessary waves to keep the radio in tune." Otherwise, we fall into the Frequential Decreasing Space and start to leave our place on the great cosmic scale.

How can we stimulate our Physical Energy and maintain its Optimal Point of Frequency?

So often we are looking for "magical" solutions to provide us with immediate well-being, and mistakenly we clutch to expensive medicines, artificial products, toxic stimulating substances, complicated dynamics, or turn to other people who promise "miracles" for fixing our ailments.

But in fact, we are the *magicians,* and the methods to remain healthy are in our hands. The key to ensuring balance is in elements generally found in front of our noses, but we don't see them... we don't hear them... we don't use them... we don't enjoy them. Maybe because they seem so simple, natural, and perhaps ordinary, we doubt their value to transform us into what we really are: simple and natural.

Let's see some of the most important and essential aspects for harmonizing Physical Energy:

a) MOVEMENT: How easy and normal is it to move the body? Movement is the first instinct of human beings and is a requirement to stay alive. It is the basic force or generator that allows the physical *machine* to convert mechanical energy into electromagnetic energy; producing the right power flow to maintain our being tune with the Material Current.

The amount of "action" we have, at a certain time, will give our organism the same internal frequency. Little or no movement forces us to remain vibrating in some level of the Decreasing Space, and too much exercise makes us exceed the midpoint and enter the Increasing Space. This is why it is so important to move in a *constant, balanced, and completely rhythmical* form; always in a sufficient proportion to keep the correct place of vibration.

People with sedentary lifestyles, which demand them to stay at a single site without much change to exercise, are most likely to become physically ill and present depressive pictures even in slight states. Sometimes we think that walking from one place to another -during daily chores- is enough to stimulate us. But the truth is that, generally, the *power load* is not enough and the corporal parts which are inactivate will be the first to display negative conditions.

Today the importance of exercise is widely promoted. Yet, with desire to lose weight or feel "very healthy," people mistakenly turn to the opposite side and over load their bodies with too much energy; again going out of balance. Let us not forget that excessive stimulation of our body can be as harmful as poor or depressed stimulation.

Then it is necessary to look for sports or pleasant physical dynamics that can be done in moderation. More specifically, coordinated movements that involve absolutely all of the corporal zones, where energy may arrive in the same proportion to each corner of the body; but they cannot be abrupt or debilitating, and under no circumstance cause pain.

Based on this, I want to highlight two activities that, for me, are the most complete, harmonic, natural, and pleasant: dancing and swimming.

- *Dancing.* Unfortunately dancing has lost through history not just its basic structure but its true function for helping our body's well-being. In many cultures dancing is disappearing, and in so many others, it has been transformed exclusively for entertainment, loaded with difficult-to-learn techniques executed by select groups.

But the authentic objective when moving our "skeleton" is to produce permanent and rhythmical energetic excitation, which maintains all the organism's pieces in their optimal frequencies. Dance offers the possibility of executing movements inherent to our corporal design in a smooth and coordinated way, and it allows us to freely enjoy self-expression and a tensionless interaction with space. In addition, the vibrations generated by the music's sound waves, combined with other beneficial elements such as socialization and joy offered by group dances, create a result difficult to exceed by any other type of physical exercise.

Dance was born with the human race and we cannot let it die. Let us enjoy happy rhythms and feel no fear when moving our heads, shoulders, arms, hips, legs, and any other muscles. It doesn't matter if we are kids, adults, or seniors; men or women; single, coupled, or in a group; if we are in a ballroom, living room, or a park. Just dance!

- *Swimming*. This is also an activity that is part of our instincts. Not only does it stimulate all of our body parts with ordered, symmetrical, and regular movements, but it forces us to breathe deeply. It should be practiced frequently and smoothly.

Just think about the benefits of swimming in the sea, where stimulating aspects like movement, water, sun, salt, wind, and sand join in a mixture beyond excellence!

Also, I recommend *Walking*, which is, without a doubt, the base of our movement. The impact of the feet hitting the ground activates all nerve endings located in the soles and ignites the rest of the organism's nerve system. However, for more effectiveness, it should be complemented with neck, shoulders, arms, back, and hips stimulation.

Always remember, the dynamism was sent to us like a great tool to enjoy, but *not* to torture our bodies. And whatever we choose to do -Yoga, Tai Chi, Pilates, Zumba, gardening, or juggling- we must express ourselves freely and be surrounded by the invigorating force of any action.

b) OXYGEN: The universe is so perfect that it makes *"vitality"* available to us only by way of an aspiration. The oxygen in air is pure energy in a gaseous state and its high vibration intensifies everything that comes into contact with it. We must get the habit to inhale and exhale in an appropriate and precise way, so the total of our organism will be stimulated.

There are hundreds of techniques promoting the great benefits of the simple, natural, and ordinary act of breathing, and we must adopt any one of them as an important lifestyle.

Keep in mind that a good "inspiration" can be a hundred times more productive than other stimulants.

c) SUNLIGHT: The powerful waves of light and heat produced by the *sun* are essential and irreplaceable to our physical system. The more solar radiation, the higher our vibrations; the less radiation, the less our matter is excited.

Our corporal frequency changes depending on the hour of the day. Noon offers greater stimulus than early morning or late afternoon, and during night the corporal vibration naturally goes down when our "smiling yellow fellow" incentive is absent.

In the same way, the lack of solar rays for prolonged periods of time can affect us greatly. For example, people who stay indoors without having direct contact with the sun -due to work or other conditions- are prone to depress their energy and enter into negative physical and emotional states. Also, in those countries that face long winters, without sufficient sunlight activation, many of their population commonly present depressive symptoms.

In hot times, the mood rises; in cold times, the mood lowers.

The sun is one of the most powerful energy activators, and must be received on a daily basis. But although we cannot be deprived of its vivifying benefits, neither should we exceed its exposure because it may also bring harmful consequences. Let's use this *shining universal gift* responsibly and wisely.

d) WATER: We often hear about the importance of drinking a good amount of water to maintain health, and these recommendations are not nonsense!

This irreplaceable "liquid gift" not only makes up 70 to 85 percent of our body, but it is also the most efficient compound for transporting energy. It is well known as a *conductive element*, which facilitates the circulation of all nutrients and fluids essential for life, and also expels toxins.

Let's maintain the habit of hydration, especially in the early morning before digesting any food. And regulate the volume consumed; because excessive water in a healthy organism can knock it out of balance, and a shortage of water may restrain our vigor… may stop our life.

e) NATURAL ELEMENTS: Every element that is part of the material world produces a unique and exclusive impulse to each part of our physical body.

Foods, plants, minerals, crystals, and all of the other components of nature can raise or lower our corporal frequency; depending on the vibratory level each has. And according to the intensity in which these stimuli occur, the sensations can be positive or negative for our body.

Because this subject is too extensive, next, I am going to highlight just a few examples that will at least provide a general concept of how we interact with our surroundings.

If something exists that more definitely influences the good or bad condition of the human body it is the range of *foods*. Unfortunately, diet is another field that has been distorted in most, not to say all, cultures of our history. We feed ourselves in an unconscious way, unaware of what foods raise or lower our vibrations; which consumables are appropriate for our age, life style, time of day, or climate of the region we live.

All this has lead the majority of people to change the body's original frequency and get used to vibrating in any of the Frequential Spaces; allowing *diseases and ailments* to continue affecting our world.

The benefits of food can vary according to how and when it is used. If our body is low in energy, we should consume products with high vibration to stimulate and stabilize us. On the contrary, if we are over-stimulated and our energy is vibrating in a very high degree, then it is good to look for nutrients of a lower load to degrade our frequency a little.

For example, to consume a very high vibration substance such as coffee may generate a stimulating effect in "inactive" people, but it can harmfully exceed the energy of those "hyperactive" ones. In addition, the strong effect of caffeine is less during morning hours, when the body is still at rest, than during noon when our internal energy waves are already high. Many goods -like industrial sugars, flours, fats, processed foods, or red wine- may lower the energy and make already depressive people feel worse; on the other hand those goods may calm, in certain moments, the anxiety of over-stimulated and stressed people.

Fortunately, ancient philosophies that use food as agents for well-being are now being recovered. According to different currents, foods can be classified as yin or yang, cold or warm, high or low calories, those that expand energy and those that contract it. They are classified according to the frequency of their colors and flavors, and recommended based on the time of day, season, or temperature at which we are exposed in the moment of eating. Equally important is to combine these foods in a proper way to keep our frequency balanced.

Aligning a balanced diet with the corporal cycles is an art that we all must learn, because it contributes enormously not only to the good performance of our matter, but also to the stability of our emotional state. Identifying everything that enters through our mouth is extremely important. We should always keep our frequency in its Optimal Point to provide the appropriate vitality in the appropriate moment; otherwise, we will continue being prisoners of diseases, pain, and toxic conditions that may obstruct our well-being.

Now, in a similar way, we can continue discovering the reactions of our body when making contact with elements like scents, colors, textures... with light, water, fire, air, earth.

For example:

- If our vibrations are very low it is better to use white or light-colored clothes to boost our energy, rather than black or very dark tones, which collaborate to decrease the frequency. Organic materials like wool, silk, or cotton generate more vibrations than synthetic ones.
- Staying in touch with living beings such as trees, flowers, plants, and domestic animals can be very helpful in raising our environmental and corporal energies.
- Walking barefoot on the ground, grass, or sand incites much more energy to the nerve endings in the feet than when we wear shoes with insulated soles like rubber.
- Crystals and minerals are compounds that Mother Nature charges as *batteries*; offering a wide and amazing spectrum of stimuli. But we must look for those that appropriately balance our energy and avoid the ones that may cause annoying interferences.
- A room painted with a cold color like "green apple" spreads a tranquil and restful sensation, but a warm tone like "red fire" produces more excitement.
- And we cannot forget some of the grandmothers' recipes! For example, the use of a *cold* ice cube (low oscillation substance) to calm the extreme vibration

of a skin burn, or a *hot* cup of tea to relax the tension produced by a stomach cramp.

Anyway, there is plenty of information for those wishing to extend this subject, especially on the internet. Material about the *therapeutic* uses of aromas, colors, oils, rays of light; crystals as healing agents; homemade natural remedies; and others offering a practical, entertaining, and, I would say, quite efficient knowledge in how to stabilize our energies.

The "bad state of health" is a situation that we humans have generated because of our incorrect way of eating and drinking and the poor interaction with the rest of the wonderful natural tools. I want to emphasize the following: *"Poor health is not a requirement of our destiny and much less a test sent by God for humans to learn lessons."*

We most please our senses, acquire good habits of life, and get the real benefit from this other part of the great *celestial legacy*.

f) MUSIC and SINGING: Like dancing, these two activities have been part of humanity since its beginning, and are other pleasant forms of stimulation.

Our body is considerably activated when we sing because the vocal cords generate internal waves with the intensity dictated by our "vigorous lungs." In addition, the vibratory waves produced by the sound of the huge variety of musical instruments can neutralize our energetic currents at certain moments.

Let's listen to smooth music when we want to calm our matter, or enjoy energetic rhythms with high vibrations -like those of the drums- if we feel down and want to reactivate our being. And do not forget the joy and excitement that certain tunes may bring when we identify our pleasant memories with their lyrics.

Rhythmic and harmonic frequencies are the language that allows us to be in tune with the rest of the universe. So even if we have a "trembling" voice, we must sing and let the exhilarating melodies touch and elevate our souls.

g) LAUGHING: Another one of the charming tools used to accelerate our material essence. This peculiar action that combines the thoracic box, throat, and lungs, creates rhythmical vibrations and highly raises the frequency of the body. Plus, the benefit we obtain from the great amount of air inhaled at the moment of a *big guffaw*.

Remember that a laugh can be carried everywhere without taking up space; we do not need manual to activate it; and we can enjoy it alone or accompanied. Best of all, laughing can be acquired *freely*; although it is possible to use particular aids like "Laughter Therapy" in which directed sessions are offered.

There are millions of reasons for crying; however, let's choose those that make us laugh... those that make us thrill.

h) RELATIONSHIPS: Intimate gestures such as caresses, kisses, hugs, or a good body massage have a quite stimulating effect, not only because they push the nervous system and heart to flow harder, but also the vibrations produced by two or more people are unified.

For example, the sexual act is one of human beings' natural activities that further boost our frequencies and lead us to experience maximal well-being; "even if only for few seconds." No wonder why many ancestral cultures -like the Chinese- consider sexuality an *art* that assures health and longevity.

Let loving, cheerful, respectful, and positive people share their energy with us.

Well! I could continue naming various aspects that influence the way in which we vibrate, but it is difficult to cover all of them. Nevertheless, I want you to remember that the physical body is the temporary home of our *being* and it was designed with the greatest degree of excellence. And keeping it in good condition offers us the possibility of tasting the freedom of movement, of action… the freedom of sensations, of pleasures… the freedom of existence.

Everything is in our hands.

Finally, I need to point out that a balanced Physical Energy is the only "admission ticket" to tune the Mental Energy; and, consequently, it will be the only "pass" to connect us with the Spiritual Energy. In the same way the development of our three essential currents appeared successively, they will decay one by one in an inverse manner, if the base of everything -the physical organism- is unstable.

If the energy is extinguishing, our body will be exhausting; if the body is exhausting, our mind will be disconnecting; and if the mind is disconnecting, our spirit will be dying.

"Life is like a game of managing vibrations that gives us the privilege to feel through the wonderful *physical shell* the infinite spectrum of the universe. And keeping ourselves stimulated will offer us a body worthy of housing a shining mind and an exalted spirit."

Memories of My Experience...

In this wonderful stage I would remember something my youngest brother frequently repeated to me:

- "Patricia, *exercise* will get rid of all your aches!"

But with so much frustration, I thought:

- "I am too skinny to go to a gym; I will probably disappear! And apart from that, what does movement have to do with my emotions?"

Luckily, later, I understood that in order to continue forward, my body had to be stimulated. It was going to be very difficult, because exercising was neither my habit nor a great pleasure of mine. However, if for many years I had had the will to take daily antidepressant pills, for now I would make "movement" part of my basic needs... part of my medicine.

I wrote a list of activities that I enjoyed, and, definitively, dancing was at the top. Few were the opportunities that I had in life where I could dance and sing, but I remembered the indescribable pleasure it was for me. And considering that *parties* were still limited at the moment, I simply decided to dance with myself. It seemed pretty crazy, but it didn't matter; I just was determined to be a "possibly nutty, but happy" person.

I looked in my house for an open and comfortable place to exercise. With happy music I developed a dynamic that allowed me to move all my body parts freely -head, neck, shoulders, arms, hip, trunk, legs, and feet- and it was complemented with different breathing techniques.

In the beginning, my body didn't respond because it was stiff and had little flexibility. So, I initiated with a short routine (five or ten minutes) and later went for longer routines (thirty or fifty minutes).

Amazingly soon, the changes were reconstructive!

I acquired agility and skill; my physical discomforts started to disappear; my body felt less heavy having more energy to continue my chores during the day; I found the desire to play with my children and go anywhere. And my senses awoke with emotion to enjoy all the things that past days stimulated me during my childhood.

Besides the movement program that I tried to do daily, or at least three or four times a week, I decided to assume the housework in order to complement the physical activity; and, at the same time, to have an organized and pleasant atmosphere that encouraged everyone in the family. Surely if somebody had peeked through the window, they would laugh looking at the amusing *dance* sessions I began having with my new partners "the broom and duster." The acts of sweeping, cleaning, washing, and organizing stopped being a reason for me to feel abused by life; rather, I began using them to cheer my life. Also, I acquired other habits such as massaging my feet, hands, and scalp; spending more time in the sun; seeking for opportunities to swim; and paying more attention to my diet.

I have to confess, it was easier than I'd imagined. As soon as the body energy frequency started to change due to movement, the *tastes* also did. No longer did I have to push myself, as before, to consume natural foods; and my apathy toward products like fats, meats, and gassy or alcoholic drinks grew. In addition, suddenly I began to reject smoking, which helped me to stop this bad habit definitively. The enjoyment for open and illuminated spaces appeared so gently; without forgetting that my closet was renewed with bright and cheerful colors. Not only did my body respond positively, feeling healthy and fortified, but I also perceived myself to be calm, enthusiastic, and less anxious.

I understood that everybody cannot be stimulated in the same way, and we must establish our own habits and speed for maintaining the Optimal Point of energy. So, I decided to adopt actions that I enjoy, and with appropriate time and perseverance, they would make me feel comfortable.

Creating new habits is a big process because we tend to return to *bad ways* that have been used for many years. On several occasions I lost continuity in my exercising routine and immediately fell into old states of fatigue and irritability. However, when thinking about the importance of *movement*, my soul was so animated and I found the strength to do it again.

"Rescuing the grand value of my dear brother's words."

Yes! Without a doubt, my great metamorphosis began to show the day I decided to move and activate my physical body. As always, I am so thankful to the universe for having given me the understanding of how to *spoil myself* in a pleasant, simple, and natural form; and why not to say it, free of charge.

Fortifying my Physical Energy ended many damaging aspects that were part of me for so long, and created a much more solid base to my personal structure. But, although this was one of my greater earnings, I had to keep strong and continue with the following step: to knock down the levee that was blocking the base of our mental expression... the Second Original Current... *the Mental Energy...*

XI
Our
Mental Energy

The Mental Energy is the universal current that offers us -evolutionary living beings- the necessary raw material for developing ideas and concepts about our physical body experiences. In addition, it is the generator of a huge range of emotions.

After birth, with external stimulation, our Physical Energy must continue rising its frequency until a certain point when a *second window* can be opened, allowing the Mental Energy or "yellow mist" to flow.

This is why, it is not just until we are a few months old that we are able to gain consciousness and discern our own body and the surroundings. Later, as the growth and mental vibrations increase, we catch more data indispensable for understanding and solving aspects of survival. And, finally, we can assimilate additional information that will help our personal development as well as our social progress.

Thanks to the *brain* (high technology material device that serves as a processor or converter) we may perceive the *invisible* cosmic waves transmitted by the universal Mental Current. Similar to a computer connected with the "Internet"; at the beginning, an initial set of *windows* appear with general guidelines for the basic system operation, and later it gives us the opportunity to search and *download* any program we want to explore.

The *knowledge* has always been in the universe. Absolutely all information concerning the complicated subject of existence is inscribed in the Mental Circuit. Past, present, and future are available at the moment we get in tune with this magnificent *celestial* memory.

Throughout history, the great geniuses, who brought forward concepts by hundreds of years and helped the world's evolution, have somehow maintained a direct link with this powerful energy that manifests in their curious minds.

It is wrong to think that the only way to *learn* about all aspects of life is through teachings left by our predecessors. We cannot deny they are testimony of the material that has been previously processed; however, we must understand that when we are correctly connected with the *original mental flow,* we open the channel to assimilate new, advanced, and more-developed judgments. And of course this is also another free gift offered by the Creator.

Knowledge cannot be invented; it can only be picked up, processed, and interpreted. And creativity is not exclusive to the most studied ones, but to those who are most *in tune!*

Now, in addition to being the basic substance of the intellect, the Mental Energy is also the producer of our *emotions*. Yes! Believe it or not, it is the Mental Current which generates all the perceptions we experience such as love, joy, security, tranquility and thousands more.

As radio antennas, each thought we have produces an *individual and particular* vibratory wave in our mind, which immediately connects with an analogous frequency transmitted by the Universal Mind. Thus, the brain receives a unique impulse that is reproduced and amplified toward the interior of the physical body, manifesting some emotion.

Just like when a piano key is pressed and an individual sound spreads, stimulating our ears; every idea that vibrates in our head touches a "key" in the cosmos, generating an exclusive "tone" to be broadcast for our "radio." In the same way, our vision, hearing, touch, taste, and smell are meant to perceive the wide variety of material stimulus (heat, cold, hard, smooth); "thought" is another *sense* that facilitates our understanding of the impressions offered by the majestic Mental Current.

The contact with the Physical Energy produces *sensations*; the contact with the Mental Energy produces *emotions*.

Finally, it is necessary to consider something very important: The Mental Current forms a spectrum of impulses and information that we catch through its Frequential Space. If we are in tune with it, authentic and pleasant emissions will be captured; but unfortunately if our mental frequency is under-stimulated or over-stimulated, it will vibrate in either Decreasing or Increasing Spaces, bringing us negative and false thoughts with uncomfortable emotions.

Our Mental Energy at its Optimal Point

The intellect is also constructed in a gradual way, and when our mental flow reaches its Optimal Point of frequency, it obtains one hundred percent (100%) of the necessary material to work effectively.

We begin handling the *"logic"* easily, which helps our intellectual development; the creativity appears constantly; we improve good memory and the capacity for learning; and the great circulation of new concepts generates questions that urge our *curious* nature to find answers and continue advancing.

All this gives us useful tools for forming clear and optimistic concepts about life and strategies for surviving, as well as for making correct decisions about any work or social aspect that will produce efficiency, achievements, and prosperity.

In addition, keeping a suitable Mental Energy volume offers us the opportunity for feeling invigorating emotions. Not only because we gained self-esteem, confidence, and security when perceiving ourselves as capable of functioning well in society; but also, when creating positive thoughts, we guaranteed a universal answer that makes us feel "good" physically.

The Mental Energy, when in the precise place of vibration, brings essential conditions for our body, our reason, and, definitively, our heart.

Our Mental Energy in Decreasing Space Levels or Frequential Depression

Just as it happens to physical matter when it is not stimulated, the Mental Energy vibratory speed decreases if we do not urge it to remain in the Midpoint of Frequency (Optimal Point).

As the mind in a progressive way, begins catching the information necessary for handling the body, understanding the environment, and generating ways for surviving; inversely, the data will be gradually erased as the flow of *"yellow"* matter diminishes.

The "software" that one day constructed our intellect starts to be de-programmed, and the "thought network" begins to fail.

When we are out of tune, our ideas become unclear and the concepts are distorted. Now the use of logic to understand the processes of life is more complicated; concentrating and memorizing is difficult; creativity begins to vanish; we feel incapable of completing home, work or community improvement projects, clinging firmly to the established ones; insecurity and fear about change appears. And not only do we lose the capacity to face difficulties, but our minds literally block solutions, so generally a sensation of hopeless and self-rejection originates.

When vibrating at low frequencies our thoughts become negative whether we want it or not. The judgments about everything that surrounds us are pessimist and discouraging. Consequently the emotions also *collapse,* being replaced with impatience, irritability, and rage. And the uncomfortable perception of ourselves makes us look around for whom to blame, and adopt conducts of sarcasm, defensiveness, and, often, aggressiveness.

Let me illustrate with an example:

During the early morning hours, I am sitting at the dining room table in front of my young daughter, with just enough time for us to eat breakfast and arrive punctually to her school. Suddenly, with an *involuntary* movement, she strikes the milk glass. It rises into the air until falling strongly and spilling the "precious white" liquid. Our clothes, table cloth, and floor are soaked and sticky.

If at that moment my mental state is at a *lower* level of the Decreasing Space, the circumstances would become unpleasant: The first concept I generate from the "scene" is completely negative. I feel irritated, my heart beats quickly and my blood pressure goes up. I look at the girl with inquisitive eyes, because I see her as the cause of an event that, for *my mind,* is a great problem. Pessimistic thoughts accumulate, like the effort needed to clean the mess and our lateness for leaving. Most probably, without thinking, I would yell at my daughter for being so clumsy, and she would cry with a fearful expression.

The time spent cleaning, me fighting with the little one who no longer wants to go to school, feeling like a victim of life, and trying to over organize myself to look well, would delay our departure. On the way to school, I would get so angry with the people who go *less fast* than we do, that I would use more of the few remaining minutes fighting with whoever crossed us. Indeed, we would arrive at our destinations behind schedule. And surely I would answer in an explosive and defensive way when my boss complains about my tardiness.

This chain of adverse events makes me feel worse. My vibrations, which are already low, would fall to even lower levels… to levels at which nobody wants to arrive.

Now, if my frequency is maintained at the half way of the Decreasing Space, my reaction would be little less extreme; but still negative:

My concept about what just happened is as a disadvantage, but I also understand that it was not my girl's fault. I *repress* my internal being avoiding shouting or demonstrating my great anger; nevertheless, I use second intention comments, such as "Why is this happening to me? Now I am going to have trouble at work; but, don't you worry, it was not your fault." Just thinking that we are going to be delayed creates anguish and, perhaps, upsets my stomach. The traffic would probably be very congested and most of the traffic lights would be red; however, I feel incapable of doing something on the matter. And, in effect, when I arrive at the office and have no courage to defend myself when my boss points to my lateness, the rage and frustration would increase.

A part of me is conscious that this state is not the correct one, the other part, is not. That is why throughout the day I would battle an inner war of feelings against logic. My vibration stays at a tension point, and I continuously make an effort to not think what I think… to not feel what I feel.

In contrast, when my Mental Energy frequency is kept in its *Optimal Point*, the situation appears very differently:

All my reactions are natural, positive, and without resistance. It is very probable that after the morning "milk tsunami" I will have a great outburst of laughter, and my little one will too. Happy ideas spontaneously appear to me, such as having a "milk war" and a competition to see who cleans and changes clothing first. My girl would move faster than ever, and we will be ready in a matter of minutes. Although it seems unbelievable, surely the traffic is fluid and we are fortunate to get green lights at most intersections. My daughter remains happy in her school. And after arriving "on time", and instead of receiving a reprimand at work, I would share with colleagues the stimulating morning I just had.

My body feels well… my mind open … and my energy vital.

In conclusion, the problem is not that my daughter spilled the milk; the *problem* occurs depending on the level of vibration at which I visualized the situation. The lower the Mental Energy vibration is in the Frequential Space, the cloudier the understanding becomes and more disfigured the emotional state appears. The personality dims with conditions that are not part of our essence such as anxiety, distress, desperation, bitterness, sadness, and hopelessness.

The correct thoughts and emotions disappeared, and lamentably the incorrect ones become a custom... a habit... a lifestyle.

How can we stimulate our Mental Energy and maintain its Optimal Point of Frequency?

Today the importance of taking care of the body is well known, but often we forget that the *brain* also has to be "adjusted" consistently.

As well as we take care of our physical self, keeping our mind in an appropriate frequency requires enjoyable conducts and activities that become habits. And again, they might seem simple and too common, but let's remember that the behaviors innate to our nature are the most effective... the most productive.

I must repeat and emphasize the importance of not overloading our energy because we will enter the field of *Stress*, which also generates harmful conditions for our mental and emotional stability.

Now, let me review some of the most important and indispensable aspects to activate the Mental Energy:

a) *PHYSICAL ENERGY in BALANCE:* As I have mentioned, each one of the three energy currents is independent but at the same time they are correlated. For this reason, when our Material Energy loses too much frequency, it drags our Mental Current to vibrate in its own Frequential Space.

Keeping a healthy and active body facilitates the tuning of our mind. Otherwise we have to make double the effort to conserve a favorable mental process (ways to stimulate the Physical Energy can be found in the preceding chapter.)

b) POSITIVE THOUGHTS: The act of reasoning positively is part of our congenital characteristics, and is available from the first moment our Mental Current enters to flow in the brain during early childhood.

Unfortunately, in a world as confused as ours, to think affirmatively is very difficult to maintain. In the course of growth, many aspects push our rational flow toward negative spaces, inducing us to create habits that keep us vibrating out of tune.

However, resuming and activating the initial attitude of the intellect is easier than we thought. Today, diverse systems that teach how to form the habit of thinking in positive are available. A large amount of books, videos, and CDs that promote self-growing and mental control can be found in bookstores, libraries, internet, and other sites. We can choose whatever offers us comfort, pleasure, and, mainly, good results.

But, I want to comment on an activity that, for me, has had the greatest degree of effectiveness, when trying to optimize the mind: "meditation."

- *Meditation* is a term for a variety of techniques used to create brain vibrations analogous to those emissions assigned to us in the great Mental Current spectral space.

Through body relaxation and contemplation on something particular such as objects, images, sensations, or simply emptiness; we can take our brain *back* to vibrate at its original and pleasant frequency.

Throughout history most cultures have tried to develop their *own* methods or disciplines of concentration and self-gathering, which allows to focus thoughts and harmonize the whole being. Many of those can be rescued; nevertheless, later I will present a very effective dynamic I call "Radio-Meditation."

Meanwhile, I may say *meditation* is the "gymnasium" for the mind to maintain its "good shape." And if it is included as part of our daily routine, like eating or dressing, it can be one of the most powerful instruments to obtain great personal transformations.

I recommend the practice of meditation in calm and natural sites like beaches, gardens, or parks. Although, the most favorable is a reserved comfortable place in our house; letting know everybody that it is our "sacred spot" and that we shouldn't be interrupted when we are there.

If we project vibrations of wisdom, we will obtain wise answers; if we think about happiness, joy instead of sadness we will perceive; if we visualize peace, peace we will feel. And if the desire is to experience any positive *noun* that can be found in the dictionary (security, patience, strength, optimism, tolerance or pardon) exactly these emotions will be part of us.

Thinking positively makes us participants in the goodness that existence offers… thinking negatively will transform us into accomplices of confusion, obstruction, suffering, and distance from who we really are.

c) LOGIC: It is the ability to make right decisions and act effectively when we want to obtain a specific result. And it is another one of the innate tools of our species, which also aids us to create vibrations equal to those of the universal Mental Energy.

Hundreds of pleasant activities -many of them left behind by modern times- promote focusing the attention on some mechanical process. Urging not only our ability to observe, concentrate, discern, and construct in a correct form; but, generally may be key elements for us to socialize with family, relatives, and friends.

Some of them are:

- Put together puzzles
- Complete crosswords
- Sew, embroider, or knit
- Make handcrafts with any type of material such as ceramic, glass, wood, paper, etc.
- Play board games like chess or cards
- Build or assemble toys

- Complete mathematical or numerical activities
- Memorize poems, tongue-twisters, or riddles
- Read aloud

Or whatever ingenious function that pushes our "noodle" to work.

The universe is logical, coordinated, exact, precise; and the frequent use of *reasoning* brings us in tune with these valuable attributes.

d) DRAWING, PAINTING and SCULPTURE: Visual arts that are also part of humanity's universal legacy.

The process of observing, designing, and constructing any project that conjugates lines, forms, composition, and balance, not only allows us to develop self-expression and obtain a visible result, but it also puts vibrations of our brain at very favorable levels.

Let's develop the ability to diffuse charcoal on virgin spaces to give our thoughts an image... let's play with textures, materials, and colors to express what our heart yearns for... let's be delighted by the view of the scene where the existence is developed: *beauty*.

Could anything be more pleasant and recreational?

e) PLAYING MUSICAL INSTRUMENTS: The action to transmit music through manual *devices* is an ancient human inclination.

The logical and coordinated process that different parts of our body have to activate an instrument -

along with the sound waves it emits- may stimulate our brain greatly and change our frequency for good.

Any of the millions of instruments that are around the world combined with singing and dancing, as I have already mentioned, can become a much more effective "remedy" than any medication.

Let's choose whichever one will serve as therapy to concentrate our mind and enchant our soul.

f) WRITING: Printing signs or symbols by hand in a rational and uniform way is another tool that has been neglected, because this action seems too normal and current.

Writing spontaneously our thoughts and emotions, is the best method for placing ideas in order, clarifying concepts about life, and helping to gain self-knowledge. And it does not matter if we are amateur writers; let's write just for the necessity to elevate our Mental and Emotional Current… let's write to bring alive the natural instinct that pushes us to transmit our experiences and wisdom through "ink."

In order to connect with the majestic "yellow" circuit, the only things we must do are: first, desire to vibrate with it; second, adopt healthy and practical habits that allow channeling our ideas with clarity; and third, be open to all information and emotions that are sent to us. We don't have to fight irrational and negative feelings; we just have to let the logical and positive ones run. Each condition of the infinite cosmic range -worthy for human beings- flows through our person at the moment a *true desire* requests to experience it.

Finally, let's remember that only a fluid and balanced mind is able to create the right vibrations for the Spiritual Energy to circulate. And it makes possible the manifestation of that wise and divine *voice,* which speaks within us and patiently waits to be listened to.

"Thanks to the wonderful Universal Mind, we have the honor of catching information and feeling sensations *beyond* the material world; we have the privilege of being conscious of our own existence. And keeping our mind stimulated is the exclusive key to opening the next door for our spiritualization and our evolution as eternal beings."

Memories of My Experience...

I had already taken the first step to stimulate my physical body. But, during this stage, I also understood that practical measures to tune my mental frequency and manage my connection with the correct cosmic transmissions were needed.

I finally accepted that thinking in a self-defeating way became a *habit* for me. And although I felt that reprogramming my brain, which had been set in low vibration levels for so many years, would be almost impossible; I was convinced if *free will* was the "dial" to change my "radio station," then my intense desire to keep going forward would be the engine to obtain it.

I swear I never imagined how easy it is to *reconnect* with the original emissions. Because when thinking about *meditation*, I conjured images of very thin, almost skeletal men, with long gray hair and beards, dressed in a white linen cloth folded like a "diaper" shape, seated in a "knot" position along the Ganges River in India or over a "softy" mattress of finishing nails; ancient practices too eccentric for me and my culture. But, now that the panorama was clearer, I verified that meditation is the most effective instrument to tune the mind, and it is not necessary to use complicated techniques... or have a "rubber" body... or be in strange places... or require interminable hours of silence and calm. On the contrary, meditation could be done effectively and easily, just in few minutes and at familiar places.

So, based on the concept of being organisms that transmit and receive radio waves, I adopted an activity that I named "Radio-Meditation." With this *simple* and *relaxing* practice of using affirmative words, I would urge my intellect to produce only high vibrations and stimulate emotions; driving my Mental Energy, again, to its natural state.

I found the best moment to have concentration and tranquility when, every night, my little sweet daughter asked me to pray at the edge of her bed until she fell asleep.

While my *Sleeping Beauty* was going into her dreams, I managed to relax my body, breathing deeply and feeling part of the silence. I thought about the "lovely" things I wanted to obtain; trying to be very specific, to receive something in return with each idea emitted.

Then, I made a list of words that form the positive spectrum and grouped them according to different aspects of life; creating one *initial or basic* meditation, like this:

- Mind: *creativity, illumination, understanding, wisdom, clarity, and truth.*

- Heart: *love, tranquility, peace, joy, respect, pardon, and kindness.*

- Spirit: *security, strength, ████, honesty, dedication, and integrity.*

- Body: *health, vitality, beauty, balance, and excellence.*

- General: *harmony, humor, prosperity,*

*productivity, communication, and
accomplishment.*

Adding many other terms that complemented the
list, day by day, I repeated these words slowly,
producing a vibration for each one with the deep
desire of my heart. Visualizing the *universal mist*
entering through a "window" located in my head and
transmitting its respective sensations, my mind's
energy frequency increased and created a tickly
feeling in the rest of my body. It took me
approximately five or ten minutes; although, if
possible, I made it a little more extensive.

I know you, my dear reader, are probably asking:
"This is it?" And my answer is: "Doing it correctly;
yes. This is it, for now!" Because later, I would
replace the *basic meditation* with a more complete
one, which would also help tune the Spiritual
Energy. And let me say, if I hadn't experienced this
in my own life, I would never believe that something
so simple could produce the amazing results that
were appearing when meditation became part of my
necessities.

Vibrating in positive, my thoughts appeared
optimistic; my emotions, pleasant and normal. My
perception expanded. My intellect was more lucid to
understand new information. I could now face the
situations that created rage and distress with
calmness and resolution, turning them into
something enriching. And one of the first changes I
noticed in my emotional state was when the bad
mood and sadness yielded to patience and joy.

As I became more confident, creative, and wiser in my way of thinking, feeling, speaking, and acting; miraculously the behavior of those who surrounded me also transformed. Thus, the interaction with my children and friends turned warm and open. The relationship with my husband recovered qualities we had lost over the course of years and new ones that fortified our marriage were gained.

By reaffirming the inventory of positive words, I created a kind of "energy quake;" a shake-up that effectively moved and rearranged all the elements of my life. Similar to when we have a chessboard and play a strategic game to obtain a skillful result; I did not have to change my "board" to continue playing, I simply adopted different tactics to make the "game" more interesting and stimulating.

I felt strange enjoying and feeling a real sense in everything that I made, and watching with optimism the circumstances that I had to face, helped me consider every moment as an opportunity to reaffirm my personality and my evolution. The "transformation" was so evident that people began to notice; perceiving me to be more motivated, awake, receptive, and, believe it or not, even funny.

I experienced an unimaginable peace and confidence in knowing that, with a strong will, all I yearned for would arrive sooner or later. I learned *to request* without feeling guilty or abusive. Better still, I understood that if I did not *wish* and did not create vibrations of my aspirations, all the channels through which the results would be obtained would be closed.

The universe waits, kind and immovable, to be stimulated in an appropriate way, so it will be able to send us the complete repertoire of its beautiful melodies. Like the keys of a piano; only those that are pressed make sound, and the rest remain silent hoping for the moment our fingers give an impulse to manifest sound.

Thanks to "Radio-Meditation" I changed my mental frequency; I changed my *radio station*. And I developed the ability to return quickly and easily to the Optimal Point whenever any external aspect affected me and threw me to low Decreasing Frequency spaces.

Learning to tune my mind was another of my enormous reforms. But I knew the last step and the final touch for a complete recovery was still missing: improving the communication with my internal guide and awakening the Third Original Current... *the Spiritual Energy...*

XII
Our
Spiritual Energy

The Spiritual Energy is the basic current that serves as a cosmic channel to catch data and emotions with much more elevated vibratory frequencies than those handled by our physical and mental matter.

In normal conditions, it is not until we turn almost six years old, when our Mental Energy arrives at a certain point of frequency that permits the *third window* to be opened, giving free way to the Spiritual Current. This powerful "blue mist" offers us three aspects:

1- Not just it enables the "Free Will" that allows us to make our first *moral decision,* but it will urge our mind to reason and question what positive or negative consequences our actions have on the rest of our life. It makes us more conscious and less instinctive.

2- It sends sensations with stronger frequencies than the ones produced by the other two primary energies. These *superior or supreme* emotions are called "values" and facilitate our interaction with others.

Thus, we have the absolute freedom to experience love, respect, compassion, kindness, honesty, loyalty, nobility, strength; or, contrarily, to move away from the central essence and experience hatred, thoughtlessness, selfishness, fear, envy, anger, vanity, pride.

3- And, to all the privileges we received through the Spiritual Circuit, we can add one more. The opportunity to make contact with the most valuable gift that we may gain as evolutionary universal beings: The Thought Adjuster.

The Thought Adjuster or Divine Monitor arrives in our mind directly from "God" to serve as a transmitter and booster of our thoughts; with the noble objective of improving our concepts about life and clarifying our purpose during the journey to a "paradisiacal, perfect, and infinite" destiny. This internal voice that serves as director, advisor, teacher, guide, counselor or compass, is not just the most-advanced tool we have, but it is also *individual and exclusive* to each of us. With respect and greatness, the "Thought Adjuster" waits patiently for its human partner to someday obtain the appropriate mental conditions *to activate it*; and this way, the *Monitor* would play the important role to link our personal energy with the Creator Energy.

The *body* and *mind* give life to the unique "personality" of each individual. And the "personality" together with the *spirit* forms the "soul", which is the special touch that differentiates us from the rest of components of our physical world.

Our Spiritual Energy at its Optimal Point

In the same way the other two primary energies manifest in Frequential Spaces and *gradually* fill our beings, the Spiritual Current does too.

Tuning the *spirit* is a fundamental element for our passing from an animal instinctive state, or simple "physical-mental" survival, to another one in which we become more developed and conscious of our real existence as individuals.

When our frequency is raised to the Optimal Point, we experience a connection with this powerful energy that makes us feel part of a perfect coexisting system and *attracts* us to continue living and progressing. It creates within us a sensation of "beyond," that, although we do not see or entirely understand, waits patiently to offer us better experiences in life. We adopt *values* that fortify our inner self and help us to humanely coexist with the outside world. The action of "service" toward others becomes an authentic reason for existing, almost a necessity. In addition, we find the strength to fight and change what we think is incorrect; promoting right and productive systems for the improvement of society.

Another one of the main aspects to maintain the *spiritual* connection is to provide the conditions for which, in a certain moment, a direct communication between our mind and our *whisperer guide* (*Divine Monitor)* may be established.

This dialogue transforms our understanding, and gradually changes erroneous ideas -acquired through our growth- into other *true ones*, expanding our conscience. This way, we visualize the importance of self-knowledge and self-control; respecting, valuing, and identifying an own character; and having the courage to follow the paths of progress, success, productivity, and satisfaction.

This spiritual vibration gives us the sensation of having a *wise company* that offers right words and emotions during confused and hopeless situations; an impulse that promotes faith in God or "superior source" that creates a worthy life for any being who *chooses* to continue the long trip toward him.

Let's remember that our Mental Energy must flow at a specific volume to generate the appropriate atmosphere in which the spiritual spark may be born. Nevertheless, if the Spiritual Current is poorly activated or, on the contrary, over-stimulated, we will begin to vibrate in its Decreasing or Increasing Spaces and we will lose all its wonderful benefits.

Our Spiritual Energy in Decreasing Space Levels or Frequential Depression

Just as Physical and Mental Energies, the Spiritual Current must be constantly stimulated, so its flow does not fall into the Depressive Frequential Space.

Otherwise, all its attributes will be distorted level by level.

And it is level by level -as we go out of tune- that we lose sensitivity to the *force of gravity* that attracts us toward the central essence of the universe. Doubt and skepticism about the existence appears. We do not manage to understand life's real *sense and purpose*. There is an impression that something "unknown" is missing, which generates feelings of emptiness, loneliness, and hopelessness. So we obsessively lean on others looking for love and support, or we give *divine* attributes to normal flesh and bone religious characters who appear more real to our perception. The less we feel, the less we believe; and our "faith" crumbles!

The altruistic feelings disappear, one by one; and negative emotions come to life, one by one. It is easy to become a slave to hatred, jealousy, intolerance, selfishness, greed, and thousands of other low vibrations that torment and obstruct the soul. Not handling thought with clarity or emotional stability, originates a life full of slips, inadequate behaviors, and sensations far from the ones we wish for. The "Free Will" system begins to fail.

On top of all this, when our spiritual foundation is weak, we find great difficulty in establishing a relationship with *the Thought Adjuster*; losing that unique, true, and immediate aid when facing our growth and evolution. We develop an insecure, skeptical, pessimistic, and incapable of facing life personality. And all these turn us away from the pathway traced and offered by the beautiful universe as our destiny.

Here is one pretty analogy that will help us to understand better. Imagine that we are standing in front of a wide, long, well-paved *highway*. It is so extensive that it gets lost against the horizon and it is impossible to see the finishing point. Next to us, on the ground, there is a wooden box that when opened, two things can be found: a *letter* and a small device similar to a *portable radio or walkie-talkie*.

The letter reads as follows:

"Hello; welcome to the wonderful world of your own existence. I am the beginning of all creation, although, at the same time, I am the finish line of all evolutionary beings of time and space. I am the perfection, the fullness, and the eternity.

As you may see, in front of you, there is a pretty road constructed "exclusively" for you that unfolds directly toward my place. If you decide to walk it, I must tell you that the trajectory is quite extensive, but full of enriching and rewarding elements. Thus, your adventure can begin with the certainty that after delighted with the trip you will be at the doors to share my divine essence.

Observe very carefully what borders the even avenue. On each side, in the adjacent lands, two great, thick, and difficult-to-penetrate jungles unfold; accompanying the main road until the end of its route, and being part of the landscape during your voyage.

While you keep your step on the presented path, you are going to experience an incessant diversity of opportunities for constructing your personality and developing, more and more, characteristics of perfection. You will have propitious moments to improve all your aptitudes and abilities; obtaining a life full of intention and accomplishment. The dreams will be approachable; the triumphs, easy to obtain. In a general environment of light, beauty, harmony, and brightness, you will meet beings filled with joy and enthusiasm who are also eager to walk this trail. And when you look ahead, and there is still so much distance to go, you will know that if you continue confidently, someday you will arrive at your final destination.

Your journey will be agile, calm, and comfortable!

Unfortunately, if by your own decision or other circumstances, you are pulled toward one of the borders and go deep into the confusing jungle; the panorama will be very different. You will face a dark, unhealthy, entangled, and difficult-to-pass environment where is no visible horizon or noticeable footpaths. You will have to constantly knock down weeds and bushes to make any progress, and without enough clear spaces that allow you to quicken your pace, it will always be the same. The dreams will be unapproachable; the triumphs, almost impossible to obtain. In addition, you will also find tired, afflicted, lost, and hopeless individuals; who do not manage to know for certain the correct direction for leaving this land that suffocates them.

Your journey will be slow, painful, and exhausting!

Now, I want you to observe the other element in the box. It is an incredible tool of divine spiritual nature and the most valuable gift I can offer you. This device -with one of the highest technologies of the universe- has the capacity to receive and transmit vibrations, like a small radio-communication device. With it, I will be able to hear everything you want to tell me and you will be able to hear everything I have to tell you.

If you yearn for an efficient guide or need a voice of support and comfort, just remember that, throughout the trip, your questions will be answered. But there is a single condition: maintain the "little radio" turned on and tuned. Otherwise, at the moment your mind lacks contact with this efficient "internal monitor," my message will be lost and you will be alone in your passage.

And no matter whether somebody pushes you or a strong wind knocks you down, or if your own desire of adventure drags you off the track; keep in mind that while the small transistor is working, you will always have the compass and the total clarity to retake the beautiful way that I prepared specially for you.

I am your destiny. You are the pilot. The Divine Monitor, your copilot. The long avenue, your route. And the surrounding forests, your option.
You decide! "

When our Spiritual Energy is out of tune, we have the sensation that we are a loose element without control wandering the universe. When we lose communication with the supreme internal voice, our heart saddens... our soul loses its essence... and our spirit stops being a spirit.

How can we stimulate our Spiritual Energy and maintain its Optimal Point of Frequency?

To experience the Spiritual Current in a true and effective way is something that has become deformed through time, because we have been immersed in cultures that seldom promote the development of self-knowledge.

Most religions continue preaching retrograde customs and philosophies that go against the real natural way. With limited, old-fashioned, and confusing concepts that obstruct the flow of progressive ideas, many young people (new generations) have moved away from the suitable habits of putting themselves in contact with their spiritual side. Do not misinterpret me! I recognize that "religion" is a fundamental part of society and can be one of *several* ways that may help people to awake spirituality; but, definitely, it must be very well structured and properly handled, otherwise, it can become a great barrier between our mind and God.

And even if we decide to be part, or not, of a religious community, yes! we must look for environments and activities that allow us to recover the original capacity to reconnect with the highest source of stimulus - directly received from the divine aid that directs our life.

Let's look at some indispensable aspects for tuning our Spiritual Energy:

a) PHYSICAL and MENTAL ENERGY in BALANCE: The first requirement to easily be in tune with the Spiritual Current is to maintain our body and mind in excellent condition.

We already know that if our mental flow is too out of phase from source, it will drag the Spiritual Energy to vibrate in its Decreasing Space. By this, I want to emphasize the importance of working the body and mind frequently (as discussed in previous chapters) in order to have the "complete" intellectual capacity to process all the new and elevated information offered to us by the Spiritual Current.

b) SELF-COMUNICATION: It is thought that getting in touch with the "little lantern" brightening our interior is only for special or chosen people; but we forgot that this celestial gift is for all evolutionary beings, or, at least, for those who have a heartfelt wish to take advantage of it.

The practice of speaking with ourselves is an innate instrument from a very early age, and this natural instinct continuously urges us to establish an internal interaction. This is why we often process, either mentally or whispering, all what is happening in daily life. For example: "Today, I want to organize my time in a better way to accomplished all the chores!" "Would my friend be angry if I say the truth?" "The neighbor looks distressed; I am going to see how I can help!"

The intimate *monologue* occurs so easily and mechanically that we neither pay enough attention to it nor realize all its benefits. There is always something to learn and something to teach with the people who share with us. But it is really the *chat* with our "I" that offers the possibility to examine our thoughts without pressure from others; to express our own life's vision without fear of judgment; and to produce suitable vibrations that will catch those universal frequencies exclusive for us.

When reasoning with ourselves, it helps not only to maintain a constant mental energy flow and to conceptualize everything that we experience in an individual manner, but it is the initial step for making contact with our Thought Adjustor. This process almost always occurs unconsciously and may seem as though we are speaking with our own person; however, if we create special conditions, someday we will recognize that the *monologue* becomes a *dialogue*, distinguishing when our mind is "speaking" and when the Divine Adjuster is.

Now, the best technique to develop efficient self-communication is through a habit that many people have been losing in the accelerated and noisy march of present societies: *introspection*.

Having a time of peace and silence, during which we manage to relax and totally concentrate on our existence is the *true key* in order to analyze who we are; what we think or feel about everything surrounding us; and which goals we want to achieve. In addition, introspection makes us conscious of the changes generated during our personal development.

All this may sound a little complicated, but, really, it is not so difficult and does not require much effort when practiced honestly. Let's look for comfortable, airy, and calm atmospheres that facilitate the informal "private talk."

Self-communication -in a meditative state- takes us to perceive our thoughts. Identifying our thoughts opens the way for personal discovery. This personal discovery generates the spark that turns the internal transistor with which the exciting conversation is settled... conversation that helps us continue living with excellent conditions.

c) PRAYER: Throughout history, every culture has looked different forms to contact the "creative force." By means of praises, worships, dances, songs, and/or rites, human beings have tried to construct bridges and feel connected with the rest of the cosmos.

Unfortunately *prayer* has also been losing its original structure and, as a result, its effectiveness. Generally it is loaded with pre-established and unclear words and ideas, which obstruct our true, free, and effective relationship with the Spiritual Energy.

If we want prayer to be fruitful, it must have very particular conditions: First, we have to believe in a superior giver of life energy, with whom fervently we wish to establish a direct bond. Second, mechanically memorized texts that lack logic and sense shouldn't be repeated; rather, we should rationally internalize and visualize the meaning of what is said. And, third, prayer must include an internal colloquial environment -even if it is directed toward an external entity such as the Creator, universe, Mother Nature, saints, moon or sun- that allows us to analyze the best way to live life. Where there are questions and answers... where clear and constructive judgments occur... where a calm communication without impositions is opened; like talking with our best friend!

I want to add that *group prayer* can be a good introduction for an *individual prayer*; however, all the participants must have true common ideals and intentions.

Just imagine a meeting where everybody raises energy praying joined hands and singing accompanied by a touching music that increases the vibration of our "beautiful" voices; an effect that connects our spirits on a glad, simple, and mainly, natural way.

d) ALTRUISTIC ACTIONS: The desire to give *love* and the purpose of doing *good* towards others are some elements that unite us with the great Spiritual Current.

"Service" is another inevitable requirement for mankind's evolution. In life, sooner or later we will face situations that require a productive, honest, and unselfish assistance to others; where we must set aside our own interests for the benefit of somebody else.

The results of humanitarian actions increase our spirit's vibration and elevate our *being* to rejoicing, satisfaction, and fulfillment levels. In the moment we recognize we are pieces of a big social system, which must work together to keep the machinery in motion, our essence of kindness and cooperation is activated. However, we must consider that the first beneficial work should be done to our own person, and subsequently expanded to others. Loving, respecting, and valuing ourselves sincerely, teaches us to love, respect, and value everybody else in a much more efficient manner.

Now, it is necessary not to confuse *kindness* with *"submissiveness,"* which frequently occurs because of fear, a necessity of approval, and a lack of security. Pleasing somebody with something that goes against our principles or emotions, simply to avoid being rejected, creates an overall bad feeling and kills the authentic sense of the altruistic action. *Submission* does not elevate the soul; rather, it destroys it!

Doing *good* gives us the great sense and endless intention of existence. It makes us live sublime emotions and it demonstrates whether our personality is progressing toward the "Divinity" or, contrarily, is moving away from her.

e) STIMULATING ACTIVITIES: Frequently many aspects take our energy out of its optimal level of vibration, so we must look for conditions that push our energy back or, better said, to be *re-tuned*.

Conditions that allow us freedom of expression and development... that make our heart beat faster... that offer joy, laughter, and excitement... that take us to feel like floating in clouds, even if just for a little while. Dance and sing at a concert of our favorite musical band or at a familiar celebration with friends; experience new places with exciting cultures; participate in recreational activities or festivals; and enjoy sporting events, where shouting and jumping with the marker is allowed. And if the desire is to do something more extreme; we may try parachuting out of the sky or canoeing in a turbulent river. However, never underestimate simple things in life, such as getting involved in the peculiar games of the happiest and most extroverted creatures on earth: children.

Let's enjoy life openly and express our individuality with respect. Let's feel how our matter vibrates in synchronicity with the universe's force.

The Spiritual Energy is the real life giver of our *soul*: this set of a physical body that contains us; a mind that interprets and analyzes our surroundings; and a spirit which offers us the possibility of experiencing life consciously. We must do everything in our power to keep the "blue mist" flowing with no restrictions and, at the same time, with no excesses; always maintaining its balance in Optimal Point.

"It is an individual decision to accept or not the Spiritual Energy's help to follow our destiny, and we can count on the "highest" respect of God and the universe whatever our choice is. But permitting this supreme current to be part of us, will assure an existence of well-being, growth, and eternal evolution. As well as the closure of the whole energy circuit that brings us *totality, integrity, and fulfillment.*"

Memories of My Experience...

Many pages would be needed to detail all the changes that occurred within me when I began to work the Spiritual Energy; and how tuning this current properly was the last piece of the puzzle that would help me balance and integrate all components of my being.

Without a doubt, numerous times I was conscious of the spectacular and *divine* presence that filled my hearth of joy and peace; nevertheless, having my body and mind so unbalanced, I felt disconnected and confused. And although I practiced "Radio-Meditation" daily to work out my mind, and a motion activity was done three or four times per week to activate my body; a habit that would generate a good spiritual flow was lacking.

So I should engage in an internal dialogue like when I was a little girl, but this time in a more efficient and definitely less obsessive way than before. And what better way to do it than *transforming* the basic "Radio-Meditation" (list of positive words) into a more personal and intimate prayer?

Evoking the experience when life gave me the opportunity to write who I wanted to be and what I wanted to live, I organized a text with logical and clear ideas; a reflection that will allow me to transmit to God and the rest of the universe who the "new" Patricia was, and which frequencies or "radio stations" I wanted to listen to with all my heath.

The secret was to vibrate with positive desires and *not* with negative memories. Without trying to find solutions for problems or putting limits on when changes should take place; I just had *faith* that creating the correct *intentions*, would cause the cosmic forces to play their part and generate determinant results. So in a state of introspection and relaxation, and with the hope of opening the windows through which the "wind" could enter and move my energies, I repeated the following meditation daily:

"I am pure energy vibrating with the creative central essence. I begin in her and finish in her. I am part of the great cosmos that sends God's light to illuminate my body... my mind... my spirit... my heart.

My body is illuminated to live with well-being! Every corner of my physical organism works in rhythm and coordination; offering me health, comfort, and freedom of movement. I feel full of energy and vitality. There is beauty, balance, and excellence.

My mind is illuminated, having clarity of existence! I understand who I am, where I come from, and where I will go. I have an intellect able to listen to the internal voice that guides my steps. I am wisdom in what I think, what I speak, and what I do; security in my decisions and certainty of taking the correct roads that bring self-knowledge and accomplishments; creativity to obtain efficiency in my home, work, and social performance. There is clarity and truth.

My spirit is illuminated and grows consciousness! I feel the universe's vigor that gives me courage to face any obstacle with calm, tranquility, and success. I have confidence that every day will occur in a suitable way and conviction that I am the owner, creator, and artisan of my destiny... of my present... of my future. There is strength and integrity.

My heart is illuminated to experience the true pleasure of life! I offer and receive love, continuously. Joy, laughter, and humor are part of my habits. I exhibit kindness, cordiality, and sincerity with others. I pardon those who have hurt me. I free myself from the situations that block my connection with the primary energies. There is tranquility and peace.

I thank God and all connected universal forces for offering me growth, evolution, prosperity, and abundance; allowing me to flow in the beautiful river of the divine current."

To close, I did a little talk with myself. Recalling what I had done during the day; visualizing my wishes for the following day; and, then, leaving my mind blank for few minutes.

Thus, ready to have sweet dreams, I retired to my bedroom!

I never thought this simple and short meditation, consciously done, could be such an effective tool.

Many new and convenient concepts arrived to me. My security and independence were improving. The route of my destiny began to appear urging me to follow it. The desire to share my history, to help others, and to give back to God were taking an unexpected force and eased my transformation.

For the first time I perceived myself *complete*. With physical well-being; with a calm, clear, and optimistic mind; with a proud and brave spirit able to change situations that I didn't like; and, best of all, with a favorable environment in which to continue evolving.

I had forgotten what *wishing* and *executing* attitude was like; but I found the opportunity for vindication. I created a "creative dance" program for children; started to give inspirational talks and workshops; and, then, embraced the great adventure of writing this book.

The most impressive ability I acquired was facing things calmly; holding the correct attitude while enjoying the journey without being frustrated about not arriving immediately to the destination. I was pleased not only with the victory, but also with the process of obtaining it; living minute by minute with the required emotion and intensity.

I must confess it felt very strange! Me waking up in the morning and feeling anguish free, with many plans to accomplish, facing the daily ups and downs with a good attitude and solutions, and being grateful for existence.

It was hard to believe the shy and inexpressive girl from the past was now stepping in front of groups of people, speaking and encouraging them to live and attain their own dreams; remembering that we are all important beings with innate capacities to move forward... that Depression is not a disease of which we are victims, but rather a condition that can be overcome naturally and effectively... that the powerful energy of the "mighty one" flows constantly whenever we are in tune.

On numerous occasions, submerged in a confused reality, I wanted to change my whole life; *be able to go away from this planet*. Luckily, today I understand that the contact with the Spiritual Energy assured me to keep the correct pathway. That in the future when I have to leave this world, I will be satisfied for having used the complete repertoire of tools my internal nature offers. And whether I obtained many or few results, what matters is my commitment and determination for being better; for feeling closer to The Creator's perfect essence; and for finishing this exciting voyage someday, regardless of how much time it will take...

XIII
Overcoming Depression

All the symptoms of Depression may be eradicated not only when each one of the essential energies (Physical, Mental, or Spiritual) recovers the original frequency at their Optimal Point, but also when all three flow in line or alignment.

Let's use a stereophonic *radio* as an example. Its "equalizer" board is formed by three horizontal bars, parallel to each other, which control different components of sound. Let's say the first bar reproduces the sounds of instruments with low pitches; the second row amplifies the instruments of medium pitches; and the third one, high pitches. (See graphic No. 9). Every canal has an interior small button that adjusts from side to side, depending on what we want to highlight while listening to the transmission. If the button moves to the left away from the *midpoint*, the tones are perceived weaker and weaker; if it moves to the right away from *midpoint*, the sound is progressively stronger.

The equalizer is used to adjust the reproduction frequencies of a range of sounds, with the purpose of matching its original emission. Better said, to manipulate different tones of the music we are listening to and play them in a balanced, harmonious way.

Graphic No. 9

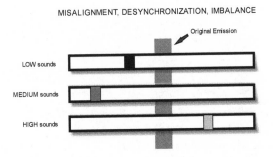

MISALIGNMENT, DESYNCHRONIZATION, IMBALANCE

The three buttons can be moved randomly, and we will obtain unlimited combinations of the same musical piece. With an *unaligned* configuration of the board the instruments and voices of the singers will be lost; or on the contrary, some of the sounds will be highly accentuated overshadowing the rest.

But if the three knobs are positioned exactly one underneath the other, forming a *straight line* down the middle of the equalizer; each part of the music will be in its best manifestation position, and, being *aligned,* the tune will sound complete, balanced, and pleasant. All the instruments and voices will be perceived clear, powerful, and agreeable to the ears. (See graphic No. 10)

Graphic No. 10

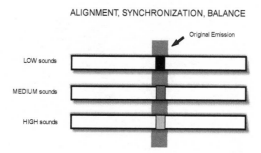

ALIGNMENT, SYNCHRONIZATION, BALANCE

Now, as radio amplifiers of the universal vibrations, we also have a *natural equalizer*, and each one of the primary energies (Physical, Mental, and Spiritual) may move independently in its own canal or Frequential Space. This way, our "personalities" will change depending on where every frequency of the *tricolor melody* is placed.

When the three currents are in *alignment* or *synchronization* we assure a vivacious and easy-flowing stream of the raw material essential for living, and our characters will be stable. In contrast, when the currents are in *misalignment or desynchronization* (meaning one, two, or three of the currents go from the midpoint frequency to either Decreasing or Increasing Space levels) the flow will lose its vigor and we will be affected in particular ways. (See graphic No. 11)

Graphic No. 11

RED Energy
YELLOW Energy
BLUE Energy

If we create the habit of indiscriminately altering the frequencies of our energies, we will exhibit destabilized personalities. A positive situation quickly becomes negative; a depressive state rises to a stressful state; or euphoria diminishes to sadness.

And although it is impossible to deny that human nature is variable, changeable, and movable; it should never fall into *unstable*, because having a bad time and feeling sad about something that marks our emotions is very different from being a *slave* to unceasing mood changes.

Another condition is when just some of the primary energies are balanced, and the others are forced to remain out of tune.

This generates individuals who are successful in some aspects of life, but mistaken in others. For example, those who keep their body active and healthy, however, they have unfortunate relationships. Or those who are excellent at work, but their bodies are heavy, painful, and their spirit holds a great emptiness. Or perhaps those who present a kind spiritual identity, but their performance in work and social environments is difficult.

The most critical part is when the three currents are pushed to vibrate *together* and *constantly* in any of the Frequential Spaces, creating chronic Depression or Stress circumstances. In this permanent imbalance no facet of life works and can take the person to limits of desperation, collapse, and even self-destruction.

Point of Balance Displacement

Depression becomes normal and repetitive when the misalignment of the three primary energies *persists* at some level in the Decreasing Space and the axis of balance moves toward the lower steps of its original frequency.

Leaving the Optimal Point of vibration for a while is not a problem, because naturally and instinctively our energy will recover and return to its initial place of balance; like a pendulum moving side to side after being pushed, which inevitably looks to return to the center of its axis.

The Physical, Mental, and Spiritual energies were perfectly designed for self-regulation; always searching to go back to a harmonic state, whenever some temporarily stimulus removes them from their balance.

By misfortune, frequently our bad habits and inadequate external circumstances force our frequencies to vibrate out of tune; creating a *false zone* of balance, where our energies look to return - actually are *forced* to return- not to the Optimal Point, but to a lower vibratory level that becomes their resting "temporary home." (See graphic No. 12)

Graphic No. 12

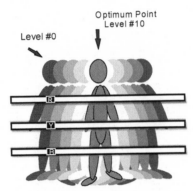

False Zone of Balance

For a better understanding let me say: if my habitual disposition is happiness (level 10), and a heated discussion with my son knocks me down to lower levels like 5 or 4; it will generate uncomfortable and negative sensations, but I can be sure that sooner or later *inertia* will make me recover the initial emotion of happiness. My vibrations will go up again to the midpoint frequency... to the true balance at level 10.

It won't be the same if my *everyday* energy states at level 4. Then, the same fight with my son will knock me down to steps much lower, such as level 1 or 0; where the negative sensations are manifested in a difficult to bear intensity. And then, although I try to be calm, my sadness will not return to the joy offered by level 10, but instead it will be forced to go back to the condition expressed by level 4.

Or, perhaps, I have become used to my energy vibrating at level 3, which generates a condition of pain, irritability, distress, and lack of desire to make physical activities. If I have a positive motivation, such as the visit of my dearest friend; my vibrations will raise several points -let's say to level 8- and momentarily my body feels more vigor, the sadness dissipates a little, and I almost experience joy.

But, what happens when my friend leaves? The positive impulse ends. Again my energies will seek the usual level in which they vibrate. In this case it is number 3 that makes me experience, once more, the disagreeable properties associated with such a low position, and not the "natural" level 10, which fills me with joy.

Happiness stops being a permanent manifestation and becomes something sporadic!

This is why commonly depressive people feel small problems are greater and more devastating than they really are. It also explains why when we open our eyes in the morning we continue feeling bad without apparent reason; since, over night, the body decreases its frequency greatly, and when we wake up, our vibrations do not return to high levels, but continue being *stuck* in some position of the Decreasing Space.

No matter how many good things surround us, sooner or later our bodies, thoughts, and emotions will be compelled to return to frequencies that are out of tune when the balance point is misplaced. For this reason it is necessary to find ways of *reprogramming* ourselves and getting in the habit of being connected with the original "stations."

Reprogramming

When we want to listen to a new radio station, the dial has to be moved toward the new radial frequency; and if we want to hear the sound clearly and harmonically, the volume and equalizer's buttons have to be located in the correct position. This way, the radio will be ready to play our favorite music every time it is turned on.

Reprogramming means not only recovering the original frequency of each one of our three essential currents, but *to keep* them aligned in the same tuned zone.

For *reprogramming* ourselves, several aspects have to be considered:

- Choose appropriate activities that stimulate our body, our mind, and our spirit individually (see previous chapters); never forgetting that they have to give us pleasure.

- The selected activities must be done periodically in order to acquire stable habits. The ideal time is every day for about ten or fifteen minutes; if a daily basis becomes difficult, try at least three or four times per week, in periods of twenty-five minutes to an hour.

- The stimulation to each current cannot be neither too little nor too much, just maintained in an average term that assures frequencies analogous to universal circuits. The "thermometer" that indicates if we are in the right level is the *positive* sensation we get when activating every current and how long this satisfaction lasts during the day. So any *negative* feeling will be the warning sign that we are under or over the right frequency point.

- Be open for personal transformations, aware of attitude changes in people around, and ready to take advantage of new roads and opportunities offered by the universe.

Whether we decide to dance, swim, take up a sport, or have a pleasant long walk by the park; the fundamental element to stimulate our body is to wake up each corner of it through movement and appropriate breathing. Complement this with moderate sun exposure; most healthy balanced diet; and, natural, airy, clean environments.

To keep the mind in shape, "meditation" will grant us the ability to replace negative thoughts with positives ones and hold an enthusiastic and optimistic life conceptualization. We may reinforce our mental skills using logic and mathematic disciplines.

And for the spirit, as a final touch, we may pray or establish a pleasant conversation with our inner voice through quiet self-gathering moments; supported with any other pleasant dynamic that allows us freedom of expression.

To diminish erroneous habits that force our energies to vibrate in low frequencies, we must adopt routines that match the complete positive spectrum of existence frequencies; assuring the correct flow of sensations, thoughts, emotions, and conditions required for our development.

"Tuning and reprogramming ourselves are the best ways to fight Depression... the true ways to overcome this condition that disable our existence."

Conclusion of My Experience...

When I look back, everything seems like a distressing dream from which I have fortunately awoken. Depression appears as a condition that was never part of me. And the veil of anxiety has been exchanged for energy of well-being, balance, fullness, and security.

It is hard to imagine that three basic aspects such as *movement, Radio-Meditation, and introspection,* today, are the base that supports the structure of my existence; allowing my boat to keep afloat and remain in alignment with the river of energy arranged long time ago as my destiny.

Luckily, I understand now that although my life has been transformed in a miraculous way, it will never stop changing. Because I am convinced that disadvantages and difficulties are going to continue taking place; that many times I will trip over bitter people, incapable of offering something positive; that society will hold absurd, violent, and destructive situations; and the thick jungles, which border my pathway, will remain there forever. But knowing that the power to counteract this reality is in my hands provides me tranquility. And whenever, for any reason, my energies leave their optimal frequency, it won't be necessary to blame others or feel like a victim, but rather *practical measures* can be taken that allow me to carry on.

This sounds unbelievable! The girl, who one day thought everything was finished for her and would never escape such a miserable situation, today, is proving the opposite. Showing that, yes, it can be done. Reaffirming that transformation occurs depending of the intensity of our desires and mental vibrations. That to produce great changes in our own personality is the first step to obtaining beneficial reforms in our surroundings, and that the decision to be guided by the internal voice will ensure us to stay on a paved road and attain gifts from the infinite. And it doesn't matter what difficult or traumatic situations push us to vibrate at low frequencies; if with true feeling of our heart, we yearn to return to the essence or departure point, the universe will be the promoter of our awakening and accomplice for retaking our celestial path.

Depression is a group of negative symptoms formed by our incapacity for connecting with the *omnipotent source,* and occurs when the natural windows through which the universal circuits flow within us are closed. It is a position out of tune and filled by interference. However, creation is so extraordinary. It gives us the possibility to come to this world loaded with simple, practical, pleasant, and completely natural tools, which can be used to get a free flow of our essential energies and to invade our beings with their powerful vigor.

We are a set of a physical body that contains an individual and allows us to experience time and space; a mental system that processes all the cosmic information, helping us to form own concepts about existence; and a heart that permits us to feel exciting emotions, inciting us to follow the route toward the powerful force that gave us birth. Without forgetting that our only responsibility, from the day we are born, is to maintain the energetic trio at the exact frequencies. Vibrating aligned and synchronized, the connection with the *truth* is unbroken and we can avoid living with distortions, illusions, mirages, and falsehoods.

And if these words sound like those of a dreamer and idealistic person I would say it is the opposite. Because a system as huge and magnificently designed as the cosmos was not created for us to live in pain, bitterness, and sorrow; quite to the contrary, it was conceived for us to cross with enthusiasm and pleasure.

Many years have passed. Yes. Many years of experience. A magical childhood. A difficult awakening. An inexplicable encounter with energies and emotions. A sea of sadness. And a consciousness that was out of reality. But, there were also times of great changes. Deep desires. New strategies. Self-discovery and self-control. Illumination and understanding. Disposition for offering and receiving. And mainly, a world of adventure.

I always will thank God for giving me the opportunity to become an *"Ex-depressive."* For bringing me the understanding that the universe is not scarce, it doesn't die, it just continues eternally vibrating. And it will never give up on us… although we give up on it.

But, at the moment of having a firm desire, we will be able to get back to feeling the power of its energy!

Goodbye
✳✳✳✳✳✳✳✳✳✳✳✳✳✳

If today you want to think everything makes sense; your life and the existence of all the elements that compose the universe have value and a particular intention.

If, finally, you wish to leave the treacherous currents that are drowning you, and move into a firm and secure land that allows you to breathe freely and opens the door for a calm, pleasant, and exciting path.

If you yearn for the energy to recover the place where it belongs; for the desire being reborn; for the joy and humor to perform their duty; and for the cinematographic tape of your existential film, leave the "pause" and continue rolling.

If your true desire is returning to be happy, you have just taken the first step in obtaining the great change. I feel proud and congratulate you with all of my heart. Keep going forward and never doubt, even for a second, that as well as I managed to overcome Depression… you are going to do it too.

Good luck and never forget:

"If the raw material with which the universe has been created is love, balance, wisdom, abundance, joy, and perfection, and you are part of the universe, not more important that a sand grain, but no less valuable than your own creator; then, how can you doubt 'you' are also love, balance, wisdom, abundance, joy, and perfection?"

About Patricia Gaviria
****

*Author, Speaker & Teacher of Personal Growth.

*Recognized by the International Latino Book Award Winning 2015.

*Amazon Best-Selling with her books in Spanish, English and Portuguese.

*Accredited by life experience she is a real testimony of overcoming Depression.

Patricia has been passionate about the reason of our existence understanding, always searching for pathways that allow her to grow positively. Since 2004 she founded a movement called "Moving Energies / Moviendo Energías" with the objective to help social integral development through inspirational talks, workshops, and personal advice.

Other of her books in English>

-*"Latest Divine Technology: The Thought Adjusters"*

In Spanish>

-*"Volver a Ser Feliz... Venciendo la Depresión con el Cuerpo, la Mente y el Espíritu"* (original title)
-*"Lo Último en Tecnología Divina: Los Ajustadores de Pensamiento"*

- *"Efecto Radio-Antena... Sintonizando Nuestras Energías Física, Mental y Espiritual"*
- *"Recuperando mi Cuerpo, mi Mente y mi Espíritu"*

In Portuguese>

- *"Voltar a Ser Feliz... Vencendo a Depressão com o Corpo, a Mente e o Espírito"*

More information>

movingenergies@live.com
www.gaviriapatricia.blogspot.com
www.amazon.com/ *Patricia Gaviria*

Your Opinion
Is Very Important
****

If you liked this book and it has been a good pathway for you to grow personally, I would love to hear from you.

You opinion is very important because it will help other people to identify how this book also may help them.

Please write your constructive comment at Amazon website where you can find all my books.

<u>www.amazon.com</u>
Patricia Gaviria / Name of the title

Thank you so much for your cooperation!!

Moving Energies